English for the Green Industry

English for the Green Industry

Jennifer Thomas

Spanish Training SERVICES

Lynn Hicks

Prentice Hall

Upper Saddle River, New Jersey 07458

Library of Congress Cataloging-in-Publication Data

Thomas, Jennifer
  English for the green industry / Jennifer Thomas.
    p. cm.
  ISBN 0-13-048043-6
    1. English language—Conversation and phrase books (for landscaping industry
  employees) 2. Landscape architecture—Terminology. 3. Landscape
  gardening—Terminology. 4. Landscaping industry—Employees. I. Title.

PE1116.L24 T48 2002
428.3'4'02471—dc21   2001059316

Editor-in-Chief: Steve Helba
Executive Acquisitions Editor: Debbie Yarnell
Associate Editor: Kimberly Yehle
Editorial Assistant: Sam Goffinet
Managing Editor: Mary Carnis
Production Management: Carlisle Communications, Ltd.
Production Editor: Bridget Lulay
Director of Manufacturing and Production: Bruce Johnson
Manufacturing Buyer: Cathleen Petersen
Marketing Manager: Jimmy Stephens
Creative Director: Cheryl Asherman
Senior Design Coordinator: Miguel Ortiz
Cover Design: Amy Rosen
Cover Illustration: Golf course, courtesy of Tony Stone Images;
Man shoveling, courtesy of PhotoDisc, Inc.; Landscaper in dust
mask and goggles, courtesy of PhotoEdit, Tony Freeman;
flower garden, courtesy of PhotoDisc, Inc.

Pearson Education LTD.
Pearson Education Australia PTY, Limited
Pearson Education Singapore, Pte. Ltd.
Pearson Education North Asia, Ltd.
Pearson Education Canada, Ltd.
Pearson Educación de Mexico, S.A. de C.V.
Pearson Education—Japan
Pearson Education Malaysia, Pte. Ltd.

10 9 8 7 6 5 4 3 2 1
ISBN 0-13-048043-6

EL CONTENTIDO

PREFACIO

FINALIDAD

Los materiales de entrenamiento en español y en inglés para la industria de la arboricultura han sido elaborados específicamente para quienes desean trabajar con mayor productividad y eficacia con sus compañeros de diverso origen. La finalidad de este curso consiste en prepararle para ese desafío. Este programa de entrenamiento le proporcionará las aptitudes necesarias para trabajar con éxito en una organización integrada por un personal de diverso origen. Usted aprenderá lo siguiente:

- Vocabulario específico de la industria
- Cómo asignar tareas, hacer seguimientos, corregir y elogiar la conducta
- Diferencias culturales fundamentales
- Consejos para la formación de equipos

Puesto que las industrias estadounidenses de servicio contratan a muchos empleados de habla española, los empleados bilingües y biculturales son muy necesarios y apreciados. Las aptitudes que usted aprenderá en este programa de entrenamiento demostrarán ser muy prácticas y le abrirán muchas puertas por muchos años en el futuro.

Los beneficios de estudiar español e Inglés para la Industria de la Arboricultura

- Mejora la capacidad de comunicación de los supervisores que tienen mayor contacto con los empleados
- Aumenta la productividad
- Mejora la seguridad
- Aumenta la retención de empleados y las referencias a otros empleos
- Fomenta el trabajo en equipo, la motivación y el buen entendimiento
- Mejora las aptitudes de liderazgo cultural de los supervisores que tienen mayor contacto con los empleados
- Aumenta los niveles de confianza y comodidad al trabajar en ambientes caracterizados por su diversidad
- Brinda comodidad y disponibilidad puesto que se trata de una clase que se imparte sobre el terreno
- Asegura la uniformidad entre el estudio en la universidad y el entrenamiento en la compañía
- El dominio del inglés y el español hablados es una excelente aptitud que aumenta el valor del currículo u hoja de vida de cualquier persona

MATERIALES DE APOYO

Para el alumno

El libro de texto incluye listas de palabras en español e inglés y las correspondientes imágenes, ejercicios interactivos para la representación de papeles, crucigramas, juegos de tres en raya, diálogos, actividades de repaso y un diccionario español-inglés. Cada capítulo contiene una lectura cultural, así como diversos consejos para la formación de equipos.

La cinta grabada en caseta enseña la pronunciación correcta del vocabulario y sirve como un examen oral de seguimiento.

Para el facilitador

La Guía para el facilitador ofrece muchas sugerencias, métodos de enseñanza e instrucciones sobre cómo llevar a cabo el programa elemental de entrenamiento. Explica cómo facilitar las actividades de aprendizaje y contiene estimulantes juegos.

- Se proporcionan **transparencias de retroproyector** para realizar la presentación del programa de entrenamiento por parte del facilitador. Se trata de juegos populares que contribuyen a que los participantes repasen el material en un ambiente divertido.
- Se suministran **tarjetas de ayuda pedagógica** en dos tamaños. El juego de tarjetas grandes permite que el facilitador presente el vocabulario y las use también en las actividades de repaso. Los juegos de tarjetas pequeñas permiten que los alumnos repasen y practiquen entre sí en grupos pequeños.
- Se incluyen **pruebas, series de preguntas y claves de respuestas** para cada capítulo y actividad en el libro de texto.

RECONOCIMIENTOS

Mi sincero agradecimiento a Jacky y Jack Thomas, mis padres, que me enseñaron el golf y el idioma español. La combinación de golf y español me llevó a elaborar este programa de entrenamiento. Los quiero.

Expreso mi especial agradecimiento a Debbie Yarnell, mi hacendosa editora, por reconocer la necesidad de este programa de entrenamiento y creer en mí.

Gracias también a TransXpert, Inc. en *www.transXpert.com* por la precisión de sus traducciones; Rob May en *www.dvpolymedia.com* por su múltiple y excelente dominio de la computadora; Chris Haserot, mi ilustrador; Bridget Lulay, mi projecto editor; Joe Drago, mi asesor commercial; and Larry Hickey por sus consejos espirituales.

Jennifer Thomas

Acerca de Spanish Training Services

NUESTRA HISTORIA

Spanish Training Services es la principal compañía proveedora de entrenamiento cultural e idiomático en la industria de la arboricultura. Se ha hecho especial mención de nuestra compañía en publicaciones como *Pro Magazine, Landscape Management, Nursery Management and Production, Grounds Maintenance y Golfdome.*

Spanish Training Services tiene el compromiso de ofrecer entrenamiento cultural e idiomático de calidad a las organizaciones con la finalidad de mejorar las aptitudes de los gerentes que tienen mayor contacto con los empleados y de los propios empleados. Nuestra compañía se especializa en dar entrenamiento a empleados que hablan inglés y también a los que hablan español para que aprendan a comunicarse con mayor eficacia y trabajen juntos con mayor productividad.

Aunque otras compañías y organizaciones educativas ofrecen servicios para enseñar español e inglés, sus materiales son demasiado extensos y en ellos no se habla de las cuestiones de administración intercultural propias de la industria de la arboricultura. El enfoque excepcional de Spanish Training Services se concentra y se organiza en torno a un vocabulario específico y aspectos de liderazgo necesarios para llevar a cabo los deberes diarios de cada uno de los trabajadores.

Spanish Training Services se fundó en 1996 con la visión de que el número de industriosos trabajadores latinos seguiría aumentando y que las aptitudes de comunicación y liderazgo eficaz desempeñarían un papel cada vez más importante en las relaciones entre los supervisores estadounidenses, el empleado hispano/latino y los clientes de la compañía. Spanish Training Services es una compañía privada con sede en la ciudad de Evanston en Illinois.

Acerca de la autora

Un día mientras jugaba golf y conversaba con un empleado de habla española en un club de golf cerca de Chicago, Jennifer Thomas se dio cuenta por primera vez de la necesidad de que los gerentes en la industria de la arboricultura aprendiesen español. Este empleado se lamentaba: "*¡Rápido!*" ¡Esa es la única palabra del español que conoce mi jefe! ¡Eso es todo lo que me dice siempre! Jennifer y este empleado hablaron acerca de cómo la ignorancia del idioma del otro provocaba una pérdida de 10 a 15 minutos cada hora en productividad al tratar de explicar una tarea usando sólo el lenguaje corporal. La falta de comunicación había provocado malentendidos, errores y la necesidad de rehacer las tareas.

Poco después, Jennifer desarrolló y escribió *Spanish for the Green Industry* (Español para la Industria de la Arboricultura) e *English for the Green Industry* (Inglés para la Industria de la Arboricultura). Ella se desempeña regularmente como presentadora en las conferencias educativas de la industria de la arboricultura y las oficinas de Extensión Universitaria.

Sus métodos excepcionales de entrenamiento y sus cursos personalizados tienen sus raíces en su amplia formación educativa y sus experiencias de vida y trabajo en México, España y Sudamérica, así como su labor como profesora de español en centros de educación secundaria durante muchos años. Jennifer Thomas obtuvo una maestría en Administración Internacional en la American Graduate School for International Management.

A toda la experiencia y formación antes mencionadas, debemos agregar su labor como instructora profesional de tenis y golf junior, lo que constituye una amplia experiencia en la enseñanza, el entrenamiento y la motivación en muchos aspectos de la vida. Ella vive en la ciudad de Evanston en Illinois y pasa sus veranos en la ciudad de Green Lake en Wisconsin.

PRONUNCIACIÓN

CONSONANTES

Letra en inglés	Sonido en español	Ejemplo
b	bandera	bat
c (antes de a, o, u)	caja	cake
(antes de e, I)	cemento	central
d	día	day
f	fútbol	football
g (antes de a, o, u)	golpe	good
(antes de e, I)	entre "ch" y "y"	Gemini
h (como una j suave)	gerente	hot
j	entre "ch" y "y"	jacket
k	cámera	kite
l	lápiz	love
m	mamá	man
n	nadar	name
p	pan	top
qu	cual	quiet
r		rum
s	sombra	some
t (principio)	taco	time
(antes de -tion)	¡shhh!	celebration
v	vino	vine
w	huevo	welcome
y	yema	yard
z	como "z" en zumbido	zipper

VOCALES

Letra en inglés	Sonido en español	Ejemplo
a	"a" en arco	car
(antes de consonante + "e" final)	"ei" en peine	date
e	entre "a" y "e"	bank
	"e" en está	bet
	"i" en mil	key
	muda	line
i	"i" (pero más relajada)	sister
(al final de la silaba)	"ai" en vaina	hi
	"i" en piña	chlorine
o (entre consonantes)	"a" en corta	pot
(después de "d," "t")	"u" en usa	to, do
	"au" en laurel	now
(al final de la palabra)	"o" alargada "ou"	hello
u (antes de consonante + "e" final)	"iu" en diurno	excuse
	"a" (pero más relajada)	under
y (al final de la palabra)	"ai" en vaina	cry

1

Los Saludos
y Las Introducciones

PARTE I   LOS SALUDOS

Buenos días.	**Good morning.**
Buenas tardes.	**Good afternoon.**
Buenas noches.	**Good night.**
Bienvenidos.	**Welcome.**
Hola.	**Hi, Hello.**
¿Qué tal?	**How's it going?**
¿Cómo estás?	**How are you?**
Bien. ¿Y tú?	**Fine. And you?**
¿Cómo está tu familia?	**How's your family?**
¿Cómo te llamas?	**What's your name?**
Me llamo. . .	**My name is. . .**
Hasta luego.	**See you later.**
Hasta mañana.	**See you tomorrow.**
Adiós.	**Goodbye.**
Por favor.	**Please.**
Gracias.	**Thank you.**
Estudio inglés.	**I'm studying English.**
Hablo inglés un poco.	**I speak a little English.**
¿Hablas español/inglés?	**Do you speak Spanish/English?**
¿Comprendes español/inglés?	**Do you understand Spanish/English?**

EJERCICIO DE CORRESPONDENCIA

Escriba la letra de la palabra en español junto a la palabra inglesa que corresponda a la izquierda.

1. __c__ My name is. . .   a. ¿Cómo estás?
2. __b__ How's it going?   b. ¿Qué tal?
3. __d__ Fine. And you?   c. Me llamo. . .
4. _____ How's your family?   d. Bien. ¿Y tú?
5. _____ See you tomorrow.   e. Gracias.
6. _____ Hi, Hello.   f. Hasta luego.
7. _____ See you later.   g. Hola.
8. _____ Welcome.   h. Buenos días.
9. _____ Please.   i. ¿Cómo está tu familia?
10. _____ Good morning.   j. Adiós.
11. _____ How are you?   k. Bienvenidos.
12. _____ Thank you.   l. Por favor.
13. _____ Goodbye.   m. Hasta mañana.

CRUCIGRAMAS

Horizontal

2. Do you speak English?
5. Good afternoon.
7. Hi, Hello.
8. How are you?
10. Please.
11. How's it going?

Vertical

1. Good night.
3. Good morning.
4. See you later.
6. Thank you.
9. Goodbye.

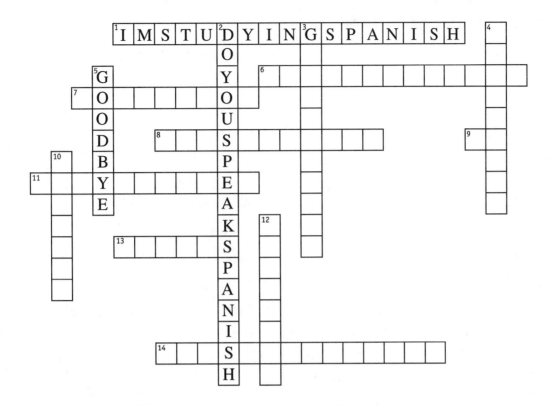

Horizontal

1. Estudio español.
6. Buenas tardes.
7. ¿Cómo estás?
8. ¿Qué tal?
9. Hola.
11. Hasta luego.
13. Por favor.
14. ¿Cómo está tu familia?

Vertical

2. ¿Hablas ingles?
3. Buenos días.
4. Buenas noches.
5. Adiós.
10. Bienvenidos.
12. Gracias.

EJERCICIO DE TRADUCCIÓN

Traduzca al inglés.

1. Por favor _____

2. Gracias _____

3. Bienvenidos _____

4. ¿Qué tal? _____

5. Hasta luego _____

6. Hasta mañana _____

7. ¿Cómo estás? _____

8. Bien. ¿Y tú? _____

9. Buenos días _____

10. ¿Cómo está tu familia? _____

Traduzca al español.

1. Good morning _____

2. How are you? _____

3. How's it going? _____

4. Fine, thanks. And you? _____

5. Good afternoon _____

6. See you later _____

7. Welcome _____

8. How's your family? _____

9. Please _____

10. Thank you _____

OPCIONES MÚLTIPLES

Marque con un círculo la letra de la respuesta correcta.

1. **Please**
   a. gracias
   b. buenos días
   c. adiós
   d. por favor

2. **Thank you**
   a. gracias
   b. por favor
   c. bien
   d. por nada

3. **See you tomorrow.**
   a. Buenos días.
   b. Hasta mañana.
   c. Adiós.
   d. Hasta luego.

4. **How are you?**
   a. ¿Qué tal?
   b. ¿Y tú?
   c. Bien, gracias.
   d. ¿Cómo estás?

5. **How's it going?**
   a. Bien, ¿Y tú?
   b. ¿Qué tal?
   c. ¿Cómo estás?
   d. Hasta luego.

6. **See you later.**
   a. Adiós.
   b. Hasta luego.
   c. Hasta mañana.
   d. Buenas noches.

7. **Hello.**
   a. Buenos días.
   b. Hasta luego.
   c. Hola.
   d. Adiós.

8. **Welcome.**
   a. Buenos días.
   b. Adiós.
   c. Bienvenidos.
   d. Buenas tardes.

EJERCICIO ORAL

A. **¡Buenos días!** Imagínese que usted está en una fiesta. En grupos de 4 o 5 salúdense por turnos. El primer alumno saluda a la persona que tiene a su derecha y a su vez esa persona saluda a la persona que tiene a su derecha. Recorra el círculo dos o tres veces usando diferentes frases como, por ejemplo, Welcome! Hello!, How's it going?, Good morning! etc.

B. **¿Usted habla inglés?** Usando las instrucciones indicadas en el ejercicio previo. Pregunte y responda acerca de sus habilidades para el idioma. Practiquen también diciéndose Good bye, See you later, etc.

PARTE II   LAS INTRODUCCIONES

Soy. . .	*I'm. . .*
argentino (a)	**Argentine**
boliviano (a)	**Bolivian**
chileno (a)	**Chilean**
costarricense	**Costa Rican**
cubano (a)	**Cuban**
dominicano (a)	**Dominican**
ecuatoriano (a)	**Ecuadorian**
guatemalteco	**Guatemalan (a)**
hondureño (a)	**Honduran**
mejicano (a)	**Mexican**
nicaragüense	**Nicaraguan**
panameño (a)	**Panamanian**
paraguayo (a)	**Paraguayan**
peruano (a)	**Peruvian**
puertorriqueño (a)	**Puerto Rican**
salvadoreño (a)	**Salvadorian**
estadounidense	**United States Citizen**
uruguayo (a)	**Uruguayan**
venezolano (a)	**Venezuelan**

¿De dónde eres?	*Where are you from?*
¿Cómo te llamas?	**What's your name?**
Me llamo Javier.	**My name is Javier.**
Quiero presentarte a. . .	**I'd like to introduce you to. . .**
Mucho gusto.	**Nice to meet you.**
Igualmente.	**Same to you.**
¿De dónde eres?	**Where are you from?**
Soy (de). . .	**I'm (from). . .**
¿De dónde es Carlos?	**Where is Carlos from?**
Carlos es (de). . .	**Carlos is (from). . .**

EJERCICIO DE CORRESPONDENCIA

Escriba la letra de la palabra en español junto a la palabra inglesa que corresponda a la izquierda.

1. __e__ My name is
2. __d__ I'm from
3. _____ Carlos is from
4. _____ Nice to meet you
5. _____ From where is
6. _____ What's your name?
7. _____ I'd like to introduce you to
8. _____ Same to you
9. _____ Where are you from?
10. _____ Hello

a. ¿Cómo te llamas?
b. Quiero presentarte a
c. Mucho gusto
d. Soy de
e. Me llamo
f. Igualmente
g. ¿De dónde es?
h. Carlos es de
i. Hola
j. ¿De dónde eres?

CRUCIGRAMAS

Horizontal

1. Same to you
3. What's your name?
8. I'd like to introduce you to

Vertical

2. Nice to meet you
4. My name is
5. I'm from
6. Where are you from?
7. From where is?

Horizontal

2. ¿Cómo te llamas?
6. ¿De dónde eres?
7. Igualmente
8. Soy de

Vertical

1. ¿De dónde eres?
3. Mucho gusto
4. Me llamo
5. Carlos es de

EJERCICIO DE TRADUCCIÓN

Traduzca al inglés.

1. Carlos es de _____
2. Soy de _____
3. Mucho gusto _____
4. Igualmente _____
5. ¿Cómo te llamas? _____
6. Hola. _____
7. Quiero presentarte a _____
8. ¿De dónde eres? _____
9. ¿De dónde es Carlos? _____
10. Me llamo Javier. _____

Traduzca al español.

1. Where are you from? _____
2. Where is Maria from? _____
3. I'm from _____
4. Ana is from _____
5. Hello. _____
6. My name is Tomás. _____
7. I'd like to introduce you to _____
8. What's your name? _____
9. Pleased to meet you. _____
10. Same to you. _____

OPCIONES MÚLTIPLES

Marque con un círculo la letra de la respuesta correcta.

1. **Where are you from?**
   a. Mucho gusto
   b. ¿Cómo te llamas?
   c. ¿De dónde eres?
   d. ¿De dónde es Carlos?

2. **My name is**
   a. Soy de
   b. Me llamo
   c. ¿De dónde es?
   d. Mucho gusto

3. **Nice to meet you**
   a. Igualmente
   b. Me llamo
   c. Soy de
   d. Mucho gusto

4. **I'm from?**
   a. Soy de
   b. Carlos es de
   c. ¿De dónde es?
   d. ¿De dónde eres?

5. **Same to you**
   a. Me llamo
   b. Quiero presentarte a
   c. Igualmente
   d. Mucho gusto

6. **From where is?**
   a. ¿De dónde eres?
   b. Me llamo
   c. ¿Cómo te llamas?
   d. Soy de

7. **I'd like to introduce you to**
   a. Igualmente
   b. Hola
   c. Mucho gusto
   d. Quiero presentarte a

8. **What's your name?**
   a. ¿Cómo te llamas?
   b. Me llamo
   c. Mucho gusto
   d. Quiero presentarte a

EJERCICIO ORAL

A. Trabaje con un compañero. Pregunte y responda: What's your name? My name is. . . Sigue el modelo.

(Pedro)

STUDENT A:	What's your name?
STUDENT B:	My name is Pedro.
STUDENT A:	Nice to meet you.
STUDENT B:	Same to you.

1. Jose
2. Susan
3. Jack
4. Paco
5. Juan
6. Jennifer
7. Lola
8. Miguel
9. Peter
10. Tomás

B. Trabaje con un compañero. Pregunte y responda: *Where are you from? I'm from. . .* Sigue el modelo.

(Pedro / Mejico / mejicano)

| STUDENT A: | Where are you from, Pedro? |
| STUDENT B: | I'm from Mexico. I'm Mexican. |

1. Jose / Guatemala
2. Susan / Chicago
3. Jack / Los Estados Unidos
4. Paco / Colombia
5. Lola / Cuba
6. Judy/ Texas
7. Ana / Costa Rica
8. Miguel / Ecuador
9. Peter/ Ohio
10. Tomás / El Salvador
11. Mary/ North Carolina
12. Jorge / Mexico

C. Hágalo ahora, usando los nombres en la parte B. Pregunte y responda: *Where is _____ from? / . . .?* _____ *is from. . .* Sigue el modelo.

(Javier / Chile)

STUDENT A: Where is Javier from?
STUDENT B: Javier is from Chile. He's Chilean.

REPASO

Lea el diálogo en voz alta en inglés.
Seguidamente tradúzcalo al español.

Mark:	Hello. Welcome!
Pablo:	Thank you.
Mark:	What's your name?
Pablo:	My name is Pablo.
Mark:	Where are you from?
Pablo:	I'm from Acapulco. I'm Mexican.
Mark:	Pablo, I want to introduce you to Gloria.
Pablo:	Nice to meet you.
Gloria:	Same to you.
Pablo:	Where are you from, Gloria?
Gloria:	I'm from Guatemala. I'm Guatemalan.
Mark:	Do you speak English, Pablo?
Pablo:	No.
Mark:	I'm studying Spanish.
Pablo:	Ah. . . yes. . .
Gloria:	. . . Pablo. . . Nice to meet you!
Pablo:	Thank you. Goodbye.
Mark:	See you later.
Gloria:	See you tomorrow.

Lea el diálogo en voz alta en español.
Seguidamente tradúzcalo al inglés.

Mark:	Hola. ¡Bienvenidos!
Pablo:	Gracias.
Mark:	¿Cómo te llamas?
Pablo:	Me llamo Pablo.
Mark:	¿De dónde eres?
Pablo:	Soy de Acapulco. Soy mejicano.
Mark:	Pablo, quiero presentarte a Gloria.
Pablo:	Mucho gusto.
Gloria:	Igualmente.
Pablo:	¿De dónde eres, Gloria?
Gloria:	Soy de Guatemala. Soy guatemalteca.
Mark:	¿Hablas inglés, Pablo?
Pablo:	No.
Mark:	Estudio español.
Pablo:	Ah. . . sí. . .
Gloria:	. . . Pablo . . . ¡Mucho gusto!
Pablo:	Gracias. Adiós.
Mark:	Hasta luego.
Gloria:	Hasta mañana.

Traduzca al español.

1. Hi! How's it going? _____

2. Good morning! _____

3. Welcome! _____

4. What's your name? _____

5. Do you speak Spanish? _____

6. Do you understand Spanish? _____

7. I'm studying English. _____

8. I speak English a little. _____

9. How are you? Fine, and you? _____

10. Where are you from? _____

11. I'm from Guatemala. I'm Guatemalan. _____

12. I'm Honduran. _____

13. Nice to meet you. _____

14. Same to you. _____

15. My name is Steve. _____

LA CULTURA: NACIONALIDADES Y TÉRMINOS

¿Cuál es el mejor término que se puede usar para referirse a sus empleados de habla española? ¿Hispanos? ¿Latinos? ¿Mexicanos? ¿Españoles? El mejor término sería el que indique la nacionalidad de cada persona. Si esa persona es de Guatemala, sería guatemalteca. Si es de Méjico, sería mexicano.

El término "*latino*" o "*latinos*" es apropiado si usted se refiere a un grupo de personas que hablan español y provienen de diversos países latinoamericanos. Es el término que se usa entre la gente. Ellos mismos se llaman *latinos* de Latinoamérica. *Latina* es una revista popular para mujeres.

El término "hispano" proviene de una palabra inglesa que significa "de o perteneciente a la antigua España." Es un término general que el Gobierno de los Estados Unidos, la Oficina del Censo y las compañías de la lista Fortuna 500 usan para referirse a la gente proveniente de diferentes países de Latinoamérica y Europa. Este término se ha hecho popular, pero a menudo no se le considera políticamente correcto.

Un término apropiado para referirse a una persona de los Estados Unidos es "*anglo*." Una palabra española para referirse a un ciudadano de los Estados Unidos es "*estadounidense*."

Los términos "*americanos*" o "*norteamericanos*" se usan para referirse globalmente a personas de toda a Norteamérica, incluyendo así a quienes son de Canadá, los Estados Unidos y México.

2

El Entrenamiento, El Elogio y Las Palabras de Interrogación

PARTE I   EL ENTRENAMIENTO

Ven conmigo.	**Come with me.**
Mírame.	**Watch me.**
Házlo como yo.	**Do it like me.**
Trátalo.	**Try it.**
Continua tratando.	**Keep trying.**
Ayúdame.	**Help me.**
Es necesario.	**It's necessary.**
Es importante.	**It's important.**
Está bien.	**It's good.**
Está mal.	**It's bad.**
Está así-así.	**It's so-so.**
Está correcto.	**It's correct.**
No está correcto.	**It's not correct.**
Todo lo demás está perfecto.	**Everything else is perfect.**
¡Buen trabajo!	**Good work!**
¡Eres muy fuerte!	**You're very strong!**
¡Eres muy trabajador!	**You're a hard worker!**

EJERCICIO DE CORRESPONDENCIA

Escriba la letra de la palabra en español junto a la palabra inglesa que corresponda a la izquierda.

1. _____ Watch me.
2. _____ Do it like me.
3. _____ Try it.
4. _____ Come with me.
5. _____ Help me.
6. _____ It's necessary.
7. _____ It's important.
8. _____ It's good.
9. _____ It's bad.
10. _____ It's correct.
11. _____ It's not correct.
12. _____ Everything else is perfect.
13. _____ Good work!
14. _____ You're a hard worker!
15. _____ You're very strong!

a. Ayúdame.
b. Está bien.
c. Está correcto.
d. ¡Eres muy trabajador!
e. Mírame.
f. Ven conmigo.
g. Está mal.
h. Hazlo como yo.
i. Es importante.
j. Trátalo.
k. ¡Eres muy fuerte!
l. ¡Buen trabajo!
m. No está correcto.
n. Es necesario.
o. Todo lo demás está perfecto.

CRUCIGRAMAS

Horizontal

1. ¡Buen trabajo!
3. Házlo como yo.
7. ¡Eres muy fuerte!
8. Está mal.
11. Está correcto.

Vertical

2. Mírame.
4. Es necesario.
5. ¡Eres muy trabajador!
6. Es importante.
8. Está bien.
9. Trátalo.
10. No está correcto.

Horizontal

1. ¡Buen trabajo!
3. Hazlo como yo.
7. ¡Eres muy fuerte!
8. Está mal.
10. Está bién.
11. ¡Eres muy trabajador!

Vertical

2. Mírame.
4. Es necesario.
5. Trátalo.
6. Es importante.
8. No está correcto.
9. Está correcto.

EJERCICIO DE TRADUCCIÓN

Traduzca al inglés.

1. Házlo como yo. _____

2. Es necesario _____

3. Trátalo. _____

4. Continua tratando. _____

5. Está correcto. _____

6. Ayúdame. _____

7. Ven conmigo. _____

8. Mírame. _____

9. Es importante. _____

10. ¡Eres muy trabajador! _____

11. Está bien. _____

12. Está así-así. _____

13. No está correcto. _____

14. Todo lo demás está perfecto. _____

15. ¡Buen trabajo! _____

Traduzca al español.

1. Try it. _____

2. Keep trying. _____

3. It's important. _____

4. You're a hard worker! _____

5. Help me. _____

6. It's good. _____

7. It's so-so. _____

8. Come with me. _____

9. Watch me. _____

10. It's important _____

11. Do it like me. _____

12. It's not correct. _____

13. Everything else is perfect. _____

14. Good work! _____

15. You're very strong! _____

OPCIONES MÚLTIPLES

Marque con un círculo la letra de la respuesta correcta.

1. **Come with me.**
   a. Está correcto.
   b. Ayúdame.
   c. Ven conmigo.
   d. Mírame.

2. **It's not correct.**
   a. Está correcto.
   b. Es importante.
   c. Está bien.
   d. No está correcto.

3. **Try it.**
   a. Hazlo como yo.
   b. Trátalo.
   c. Continua tratando.
   d. Ayúdame.

4. **Watch me.**
   a. Está correcto.
   b. Ayúdame.
   c. Ven conmigo.
   d. Mírame.

5. **Help me.**
   a. Está correcto.
   b. Ayúdame.
   c. Ven conmigo.
   d. Mírame.

6. **It's important.**
   a. Está correcto.
   b. Es importante.
   c. Está bien.
   d. No está correcto.

7. **You're a hard worker!**
   a. ¡Eres muy trabajador!
   b. No está correcto.
   c. Todo lo demás está perfecto.
   d. ¡Buen trabajo!

8. **Good work!**
   a. No está correcto.
   b. ¡Eres muy fuerte!
   c. ¡Buen trabajo!
   d. ¡Eres muy trabajador!

9. **Keep trying.**
   a. Hazlo como yo.
   b. Trátalo.
   c. Continua tratando.
   d. Ayúdame.

10. **Do it like me.**
    a. Hazlo como yo.
    b. Trátalo.
    c. Continua tratando.
    d. Ayúdame.

PARTE II   EL ELOGIO

¡Perfecto!	**Perfect!**	¡Fabuloso!	**Fabulous!**
¡Increíble!	**Incredible!**	¡Fantástico!	**Fantastic!**
¡Excelente!	**Excellent!**	¡Magnífico!	**Magnificent!**
¡Excepcional!	**Exceptional!**	¡Maravilloso!	**Marvelous!**

EJERCICIO DE CORRESPONDENCIA

Escriba la letra de la palabra en español junto a la palabra inglesa que corresponda a la izquierda.

1. _____ Perfect!   a. ¡Excepcional!
2. _____ Incredible!   b. ¡Fabuloso!
3. _____ Excellent!   c. ¡Fantástico!
4. _____ Exceptional!   d. ¡Perfecto!
5. _____ Fabulous!   e. ¡Maravilloso!
6. _____ Fantastic!   f. ¡Excelente!
7. _____ Magnificent!   g. ¡Increíble!
8. _____ Marvelous!   h. ¡Magnífico!

CRUCIGRAMAS

Horizontal

3. Exceptional
5. Magnificent
7. Perfect

Vertical

1. Fantastic
2. Incredible
3. Excellent
4. Marvelous
6. Fabulous

Horizontal

3. Excelente
6. Maravilloso
7. Fabuloso
8. Perfecto

Vertical

1. Excepcional
2. Increíble
4. Fantástico
5. Magnífico

PARTE III   EL INTERROGACIÓN

Dónde	**Where**
Dónde está	**Where is**
Cuándo	**When**
Qué	**What**
Quién	**Who**
Con quién	**With whom**
Por qué	**Why**
Cómo	**How**
Cuántos	**How many**

EJERCICIO DE CORRESPONDENCIA

Escriba la letra de la palabra en español junto a la palabra inglesa que corresponda a la izquierda.

1. _____ When
2. _____ What
3. _____ How many
4. _____ Where is
5. _____ Who

6. _____ Where
7. _____ With whom
8. _____ Why
9. _____ How

a. Cuántos
b. Quién
c. Con quién
d. Cómo
e. Qué

f. Cuándo
g. Por qué
h. Dónde
i. Dónde está

CRUCIGRAMAS

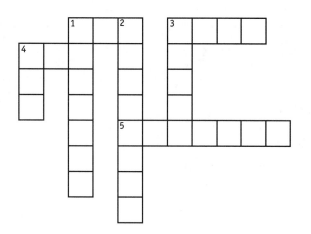

Horizontal

1. Cómo
3. Cuándo
4. Quién
5. Dónde está

Vertical

1. Cuántos
2. Con quién
3. Dónde
4. Por qué

Horizontal

2. How
4. Where
6. What
9. Where is

Vertical

1. Why
3. With whom
5. When
7. How many
8. Who

EJERCICIO DE TRADUCCIÓN

Traduzca al inglés.

1. Dónde _____

2. Cuándo _____

3. Quién_____

4. Dónde está_____

5. Con quién _____

6. Por qué _____

7. Cuántos _____

8. Qué _____

9. Cómo_____

Traduzca al español.

1. Who_____

2. Where _____

3. How many_____

4. When_____

5. Where is_____

6. With whom _____

7. Why_____

8. How_____

9. What _____

OPCIONES MÚLTIPLES

Marque con un círculo la letra de la respuesta correcta.

1. **When**
   a. Dónde
   b. Quién
   c. Qué
   d. Cuándo

2. **Where is**
   a. Con quién
   b. Por qué
   c. Dónde está
   d. Cómo

3. **Who**
   a. Cuántos
   b. Quién
   c. Qué
   d. Cuándo

4. **With whom**
   a. Con quién
   b. Por qué
   c. Dónde está
   d. Cómo

5. **What**
   a. Dónde
   b. Quién
   c. Qué
   d. Cuándo

6. **How**
   a. Con quién
   b. Por qué
   c. Dónde está
   d. Cómo

7. **Where**
   a. Dónde
   b. Quién
   c. Qué
   d. Cuándo

8. **How many**
   a. Quién
   b. Cuántos
   c. Qué
   d. Cuándo

9. **Why**
   a. Con quién
   b. Por qué
   c. Dónde está
   d. Cómo

REPASO

Lea el diálogo en voz alta en español.
Seguidamente tradúzcalo al inglés.

Jacky: ¡Hola Pablo!

Pablo: Buenos días.

Jacky: ¿Cómo estás?

Pablo: Bien, gracias.

Jacky: Por favor... Ven conmigo.

Pablo: Okay.

Jacky: Es importante... Mírame.

Pablo: (mira a Jacky)

Jacky: Trátalo.

Pablo: (lo trata... pero no tiene much confianza)

Jacky: Házlo como yo.

Pablo: No está correcto...

Jacky: Continua tratando.

Pablo: (trata otra vez...)

Jacky: ¡Excelente!

Pablo: ¿Está bien?

Jacky: Sí. Todo lo demás está perfecto.

Pablo: (tiene mucho orgullo)

Jacky: Gracias. ¡Eres muy trabajador!

Lea el diálogo en voz alta en inglés.
Seguidamente tradúzcalo al español.

Jacky: Hello Pablo!

Pablo: Good morning.

Jacky: How are you?

Pablo: Fine, thank you.

Jacky: Please... Come with me.

Pablo: Okay.

Jacky: It's important... Watch me.

Pablo: (watches Jacky)

Jacky: Try it.

Pablo: (tries it... but is not very confident)

Jacky: Do it like me.

Pablo: It's not correct...

Jacky: Keep trying.

Pablo: (tries it again...)

Jacky: Excellent!

Pablo: It's good?

Jacky: Yes. Everything else is perfect.

Pablo: (he is very proud)

Jacky: Thank you. You're a hard worker!

Traduzca al español.

1. It's important. _____

2. It's necessary. _____

3. Come with me. _____

4. Do it like me. _____

5. Perfect! _____

6. Fantastic! _____

7. Try it. _____

8. You're very strong! _____

9. It's good. It's bad. _____

10. It's correct. It's not correct. _____

11. Everything else is perfect. _____

12. You're a hard worker! _____

13. Marvelous! _____

14. Help me. _____

15. Where is _____

16. Who _____

17. With whom _____

18. How many _____

19. Where _____

20. When _____

21. Please _____

22. Thank you _____

23. Welcome _____

24. How's it going? _____

25. What's your name? _____

26. My name is Rich. _____

27. Do you speak English? _____

28. I'm studying Spanish. _____

29. Where are you from? _____

30. I'm from Bolivia. I'm Bolivian. _____

31. Nice to meet you. _____

32. Where is Jesús from? _____

33. Jesús is from Guadalajara. _____

34. I'd like to introduce you to _____

35. See you later. _____

LA CULTURA: SENSIBILIDADES CULTURALES

Los hombres estadounidenses han sido condicionados desde su infancia a ocultar sus emociones, porque se considera que mostrarlas es una señal de debilidad. Como adultos, ellos traen esta actitud al mundo del trabajo y los negocios "guardando la compostura" y dando la impresión de ser imperturbables. La tenacidad y la testarudez son cualidades respetadas y admiradas. Por lo general se comprende que las emociones y los negocios no son una buena combinación; ésto permite que los gerentes de los Estados Unidos acepten críticas a su trabajo y aprendan de sus errores, sin tomarse las críticas como algo personal. En los Estados Unidos es importante recordar que en los negocios al criticar el trabajo de alguien, no se está criticando personalmente a nadie.

Los trabajadores estadounidenses suprimen cualquier rasgo de sensibilidad que puedan sentir. Todos los días de trabajo podemos ver abundantes ejemplos de esta actitud endurecida. Un superior puede increpar a un subordinado con bastante severidad por un error que el subordinado haya cometido, pero no sería raro verlos un rato después riéndose juntos mientras toman una taza de café. Todo se olvida y su relación personal es tan cordial como antes. En dos palabras, las emociones se consideran como algo personal, como algo que no tiene razón de ser en el duro mundo de los negocios.

Los latinos son sumamente sensibles a las críticas debido a una respuesta emocional a todo lo que los afecte personalmente. Esto incluye las críticas a su trabajo. Se sienten orgullosos de su trabajo y lo demuestran. Cuando se critica su trabajo, los latinos se toman esa crítica como algo personal. Cuando se les critica, se sienten ofendidos y con frecuencia evitarán el trato personal con la persona que los haya criticado. A menudo dejan de hablarle a esa persona o la tratan con frialdad o le responden con el silencio. Debido a esta sensibilidad, muchas veces la gente piensa que los latinos son "susceptibles."

3

Los Números, El Calendario y El Tiempo

PARTE I   LOS NÚMEROS

Cardinales

0	**zero**	13	**thirteen**	25	**twenty five**	80	**eighty**
1	**one**	14	**fourteen**	26	**twenty six**	90	**ninety**
2	**two**	15	**fifteen**	27	**twenty seven**	100	**one hundred**
3	**three**	16	**sixteen**	28	**twenty eight**	200	**two hundred**
4	**four**	17	**seventeen**	29	**twenty nine**	300	**three hundred**
5	**five**	18	**eighteen**	30	**thirty**	400	**four hundred**
6	**six**	19	**nineteen**	31	**thirty one**	500	**five hundred**
7	**seven**	20	**twenty**	32	**thirty two**	600	**six hundred**
8	**eight**	21	**twenty one**	40	**forty**	700	**seven hundred**
9	**nine**	22	**twenty two**	50	**fifty**	800	**eight hundred**
10	**ten**	23	**twenty three**	60	**sixty**	900	**nine hundred**
11	**eleven**	24	**twenty four**	70	**seventy**	1000	**one thousand**
12	**twelve**						

Ordinales

primero	**first**
segundo	**second**
tercero	**third**

EJERCICIO DE CORRESPONDENCIA

Escriba la letra de la palabra en español junto a la palabra inglesa que corresponda a la izquierda.

1. ____ 6	10. ____ 3	a. trece	j. diez y ocho
2. ____ 14	11. ____ 12	b. cero	k. uno
3. ____ 8	12. ____ 11	c. diez	l. quince
4. ____ 10	13. ____ 1	d. nueve	m. doce
5. ____ 15	14. ____ 16	e. diez y siete	n. catorce
6. ____ 0	15. ____ 9	f. seis	o. ocho
7. ____ 7	16. ____ 17	g. cuatro	p. dos
8. ____ 18	17. ____ 13	h. diez y seis	q. once
9. ____ 2	18. ____ 4	i. tres	r. siete

EJERCICIO DE CORRESPONDENCIA

Escriba la letra de la palabra en español junto a la palabra inglesa que corresponda a la izquierda.

1. ____ 20	6. ____ 40	a. treinta	f. diez
2. ____ 70	7. ____ 90	b. noventa	g. veinte
3. ____ 10	8. ____ 30	c. sesenta	h. cien
4. ____ 80	9. ____ 60	d. setenta	i. cincuenta
5. ____ 100	10. ____ 50	e. ochenta	j. cuarenta

OPCIONES MÚLTIPLES

Marque con un círculo la letra de la respuesta correcta.

1. 80
a. eight hundred
b. eighty
c. eight
d. eighteen

2. 9
a. nine
b. nine hundred
c. ninety
d. nineteen

3. 100
a. ten
b. one
c. one hundred
d. eleven

4. 2
a. two
b. one
c. twenty
d. twelve

5. 300
a. thirty
b. three
c. thirteen
d. three hundred

6. 50
a. fifteen
b. fifty
c. five
d. five hundred

7. 3
a. three
b. thirty
c. thirteen
d. three hundred

8. 18
a. eight
b. eighteen
c. eighty
d. eight hundred

9. 20
a. twenty two
b. twelve
c. twenty
d. thirty

10. 14
a. four
b. fourteen
c. forty
d. four hundred

EJERCICIO DE ROLE PLAY

A. **El teléfono.** Su profesor(a) leerá algunos de sus números telefónicos. Levante la mano y responda "Hello" cuando escuche su número.

B. **¡Muchos números!** Su organización tiene ahora una nueva sistema telefónico. Túrnese con su compañero para decir: *My telephone / fax / cell number is...*

Tom Wright

The Design Build Company
6960 Central Avenue

Tel: 233 - 565 - 2266
Fax: 233 - 565 - 2263
Cell: 919 - 929 - 0011

Howard King

Lang Landscape Company
3021 Oak Street

Tel: 233 - 560 - 2100
Fax: 233 - 560 - 2199
Cell: 919 - 924 - 4568

Mark Huston

Wilmette Golf and Tennis Club
70247 River Road

Tel: 448 - 513 - 4646
Fax: 448 - 513 - 4648
Cell: 770 - 808 - 3738

Peg O' Callahan

Blue Lake Nursery
55086 Highway 23

Tel: 707 - 234 - 8949
Fax: 707 - 234 - 8948
Cell: 292 - 876 - 0606

C. **Mi número es...** Cada alumno debe preguntar al siguiente compañero cuál es su número telefónico. Otro alumno debe anotar los números en la pizarra. Si el alumno que está anotando los números comete un error, el alumno cuyo número está anotando debe corregirlo y seguidamente tomar el puesto del anotador en la pizarra.

STUDENT A: What's your telephone / fax / cell number?
STUDENT B: My _____ number is...

D. **Las direcciones.** Imagínese que su compañero es su empleado. Usando las tarjetas de visita, dígale que vaya a trabajar a esas direcciones. Use *Go to...* *(Vete a...)* Seguidamente trate de expresar first *(primero)* and second *(segundo)* con los locales comerciales.

LA GRAMÁTICA: HAY

Hay significa "there is" o "there are."

Hay una fiesta.	**There's a party.**
Hay diez pizzas.	**There are ten pizzas.**

En una pregunta, *Hay* significa "Is there. . .?" o "Are there. . .?"

¿Hay cerveza?	**Is there beer?**
¿Hay discos?	**Are there CDs?**

No hay significa "there isn't any" o "there aren't any." En una pregunta significa "Isn't there any?" o "Aren't there any?"

No hay música.	**There isn't any music.**
No hay pizzas.	**There aren't any pizzas.**
¿No hay música?	**Isn't there any music?**
¿No hay pizzas?	**Aren't there any pizzas?**

Usamos *How many?* para preguntar cuantas cosas hay. A veces *a little* y *a few* están usados en la respuesta.

¿Cuántos tacos hay?	**How many tacos are there?**
Hay treinta.	**There are thirty.**
Hay muchos.	**There are a lot.**
¿Cuántas pizzas hay?	**How many pizzas are there?**
Hay tres.	**There are three.**
Hay pocas.	**There are a few.**

EJERCICIO DE TRADUCCIÓN

Traduzca al inglés.

1. Hay una fiesta. _____

2. Hay pizza. _____

3. No hay cerveza. _____

4. No hay música. _____

5. ¿Cuántos tacos hay? _____

6. ¿Cuántos burritos hay? _____

7. ¿No hay pizza? _____

8. Hay seis. _____

9. Hay pocos. _____

10. Hay muchos. _____

Traduzca al español.

1. There is a party. _____

2. There is beer. _____

3. There is no pizza. _____

4. There is no music. _____

5. How many tacos are there? _____

6. How many burritos are there? _____

7. There are eight. _____

8. There are a lot of parties. _____

9. There are few pizzas. _____

10. Is there a lot of beer? _____

EJERCICIO DE ROLE PLAY

A. **¿Muchos o pocos?** Su compañía le ha pedido a usted y a un compañero de trabajo que ayuden a preparar la cena de bienvenida que la compañía está organizando para sus nuevos empleados. Dígale a su compañero si hay muchos o sólo pocos de los artículos mostrados. (Considere que todas las cosas de las que haya menos de seis unidades son pocas.)

hamburgers	tacos
beers	burritos
plates	pizzas
sandwiches	salads

B. **¿Cuántos hay?** Usando la foto en el ejercicio de práctica A, túrnese con un compañero para preguntar y responder cuántas unidades de cada foto hay sobre la mesa.

STUDENT A: How many burritos are there?

STUDENT B: There are eight.

PARTE II   EL CALENDARIO

Las Estaciones – Seasons

la primavera
spring

el verano
summer

el otoño
fall

el invierno
winter

Los Meses del Año – Months of the Year

enero	**January**	julio	**July**
febrero	**February**	agosto	**August**
marzo	**March**	septiembre	**September**
abril	**April**	octubre	**October**
mayo	**May**	noviembre	**November**
junio	**June**	diciembre	**December**

Los Días de la Semana — Days of the Week

el domingo	**Sunday**	el jueves	**Thursday**
el lunes	**Monday**	el viernes	**Friday**
el martes	**Tuesday**	el sábado	**Saturday**
el miércoles	**Wednesday**		

Otras Palabras — Other Words

el día	**day**	mañana por la mañana	**tomorrow morning**
la semana	**week**	mañana por la tarde	**tomorrow afternoon**
el mes	**month**	mañana por la noche	**tomorrow night**
el fin de semana	**weekend**	cada mañana	**every morning**
el año	**year**	cada día	**every day**
hoy	**today**	cada tarde	**every afternoon**
mañana	**tomorrow**	cada noche	**every night**
ayer	**yesterday**		
		todo el tiempo	**all the time**
mañana	**morning**	solamente	**only**
tarde	**afternoon**	nunca	**never**
noche	**night**		

EJERCICIO DE CORRESPONDENCIA

Escriba la letra de la palabra en español junto a la palabra inglesa que corresponda a la izquierda.

1. ____ November	9. ____ February	a. mayo	i. agosto
2. ____ July	10. ____ October	b. febrero	j. julio
3. ____ January	11. ____ summer	c. invierno	k. primavera
4. ____ August	12. ____ spring	d. junio	l. marzo
5. ____ fall	13. ____ April	e. abril	m. verano
6. ____ September	14. ____ May	f. octubre	n. otoño
7. ____ June	15. ____ March	g. noviembre	o. enero
8. ____ winter	16. ____ December	h. diciembre	p. septiembre

CRUCIGRAMAS

Horizontal

6. September
7. April
8. March
9. October
11. January
12. July

Vertical

1. November
2. August
3. December
4. February
5. May
10. June

Horizontal

2. junio
3. marzo
5. abril
7. enero
9. septiembre
10. noviembre
11. octubre

Vertical

1. febrero
3. mayo
4. julio
6. agosto
8. diciembre

EJERCICIO DE TRADUCCIÓN

Traduzca al español.

1. February _____

2. April _____

3. May _____

4. June _____

5. August _____

6. October _____

7. November _____

8. January _____

9. March _____

10. July _____

11. September _____

12. December _____

Traduzca al español.

1. spring _____

3. fall _____

2. summer _____

4. winter _____

EJERCICIO DE ROLE PLAY

A. **¡Día de paga!** Para la planificación financiera, su organización ha repartido un calendario en el que se señalan los días de paga. Indique las fechas trabajando en equipo con un compañero. Sigue el modelo.

(5 de mayo, 15 de mayo)

| STUDENT A: | May 5 |
| STUDENT B: | May 15 |

enero 10, 24	julio 12, 28
febrero 8, 22	agosto 8, 31
marzo 2, 13	septiembre 17, 29
abril 6, 19	octubre 9, 19
mayo 10, 24	noviembre 4, 14
junio 16, 30	diciembre 3, 13

B. **¿Cuando es tu cumpleaños?** Trabaje en grupo, preguntando y respondiendo cuándo es el día de cumpleaños de cada uno. Sigue el modelo.

| STUDENT A: | When is your birthday? |
| STUDENT B: | My birthday is May 3. |

C. **Forme una fila.** Trabaje con toda la clase. Pregúntense entre sí: "When is your birthday?" y espere la respuesta "My birthday is. . ." Forme una fila según el orden de sus cumpleaños comenzando con el 1 de enero y terminando con el 31 de diciembre. Compruebe si formaron correctamente la fila pidiéndole a quien tenga el primer cumpleaños en enero que diga en voz alta su fecha en inglés y así sucesivamente hasta decir todos los cumpleaños de los compañeros en la fila.

EJERCICIO DE CORRESPONDENCIA

Escriba la letra de la palabra en español junto a la palabra inglesa que corresponda a la izquierda.

1. _____ Friday
2. _____ Tuesday
3. _____ Saturday
4. _____ Thursday
5. _____ Sunday
6. _____ Wednesday
7. _____ Monday
8. _____ day

9. _____ month
10. _____ week
11. _____ year
12. _____ today
13. _____ tomorrow
14. _____ weekend
15. _____ yesterday

a. hoy
b. lunes
c. sábado
d. miércoles
e. año
f. martes
g. viernes
h. ayer

i. fin de semana
j. jueves
k. domingo
l. semana
m. mañana
n. día
o. mes

CRUCIGRAMAS

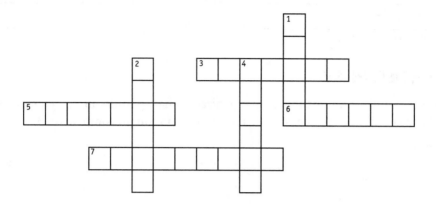

Horizontal

3. Sunday
5. Friday
6. Saturday
7. Wednesday

Vertical

1. Monday
2. Thursday
4. Tuesday

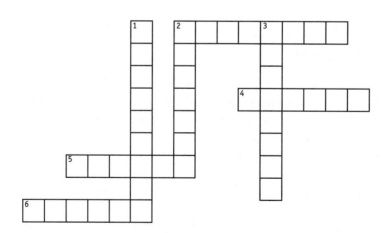

Horizontal

2. jueves
4. domingo
5. lunes
6. viernes

Vertical

1. miércoles
2. martes
3. sábado

EJERCICIO DE TRADUCCIÓN

Traduzca al español.

1. Sunday _____

2. Friday _____

3. Thursday _____

4. Monday _____

5. Saturday _____

6. Tuesday _____

7. Wednesday _____

Traduzca al español.

1. today _____

2. tomorrow _____

3. morning _____

4. afternoon _____

5. day _____

6. weekend _____

7. everyday _____

8. every afternoon _____

9. every morning _____

10. only _____

OPCIONES MÚLTIPLES

Marque con un círculo la letra de la respuesta correcta.

1. **Sunday**
   a. domingo
   b. sábado
   c. jueves
   d. viernes

2. **Friday**
   a. martes
   b. jueves
   c. viernes
   d. domingo

3. **Wednesday**
   a. sábado
   b. lunes
   c. jueves
   d. miércoles

4. **Tuesday**
   a. domingo
   b. jueves
   c. viernes
   d. martes

5. **Monday**
   a. sábado
   b. lunes
   c. jueves
   d. miércoles

6. **Thursday**
   a. domingo
   b. jueves
   c. viernes
   d. martes

7. **Saturday**
   a. sábado
   b. lunes
   c. domingo
   d. miércoles

EJERCICIO ORAL

Vaya a... imagínese que su compañero de clase es su compañero de trabajo. Usando *Go to...Vete...*túrnense para decire dónde deben ir en los días indicados. Para expresar "*el*" use la palabra inglesa "*on*." Sigue el modelo.

1195 Asbury Street (lunes-martes)
Go to 1195 Asbury on Monday and Tuesday.

1. 2303 Madison Street (lunes-miércoles-viernes)
2. 369 Brown Avenue (martes-jueves)
3. 5500 Route 43 (lunes-martes-miércoles)
4. 450 Highway 83 (jueves-viernes-sábado)
5. Number 16, 17, 18 (lunes-miércoles-viernes)

6. 290 Sassafras Road (lunes-jueves-sábado)
7. 700 Highway 55 (viernes-sábado)
8. 782 Hinman Street (lunes-miércoles-viernes)
9. 9115 Hunter Boulevard (martes-jueves-viernes)
10. Number 7, 8, 9 (martes-sábado)

PARTE III   EL TIEMPO

Para aprender como expresar la hora en inglés, estudie los ejemplos.

La hora en punto:

1:00	Es la una.	**It's one o'clock.**
2:00	Son las dos.	**It's two o'clock.**
7:00	Son las siete.	**It's seven o'clock.**

Después de la hora en punto:

1:10	Es la una y diez.	**It's one ten.**
2:20	Son las dos y veinte.	**It's two-twenty.**
3:15	Son las tres y cuarto.	**It's three fifteen.**
	(o Son las tres y quince.)	
5:30	Son las cinco y media.	**It's five thirty.**
	(o Son las cinco y treinta.)	

Antes de la hora en punto:

6:55	Son las siete menos cinco.	**It's five to seven.**
3:45	Son las cuatro menos quince.	**It's three forty-five.**
	(o Son las cuatro menos cuarto.)	

A las ocho. . . A las nueve, etc., sería at eight, at nine, etc.

¿A qué hora es...?	**At what time is...?**
¿A qué hora es la fiesta?	**At what time is the party?**
La fiesta es a las seis.	**The party is at 6:00.**

Expresiones de tiempo

¿Qué hora es?	**What time is it?**	por la noche	**at night**
Son las cinco.	**It's five o'clock.**	a tiempo	**on time**
¿A qué hora es...?	**At what time is...**	en punto	**exactly, sharp**
A las dos, tres...	**At 2:00, 3:00...**	tarde	**late**
por la mañana	**in the morning**	temprano	**early**
por la tarde	**in the afternoon**	todo el tiempo	**all the time**

EJERCICIO DE CORRESPONDENCIA

Escriba la letra de la palabra en español junto a la palabra inglesa que corresponda a la izquierda.

1. _____ It's 2:00.
2. _____ At 2:00
3. _____ It's 10:00.
4. _____ At 10:00
5. _____ What time is it?
6. _____ It's 6:30.
7. _____ At 6:30

8. _____ At what time is?
9. _____ in the morning
10. _____ in the afternoon
11. _____ early
12. _____ late
13. _____ on time
14. _____ exactly, sharp

a. temprano
b. A las dos
c. Son las diez.
d. A tiempo
e. ¿Qué hora es?
f. Son las dos.
g. tarde

h. en punto
i. Son las seis y media.
j. A las diez
k. de la tarde
l. ¿A qué hora es?
m. de la mañana
n. A las seis y media

CRUCIGRAMAS

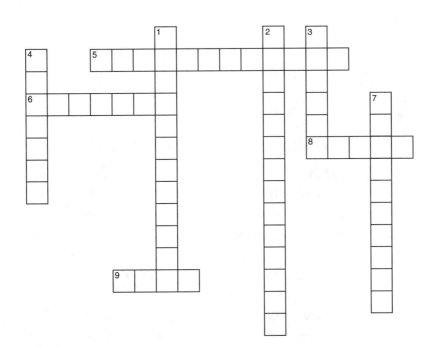

Horizontal

5. por la mañana
6. por la noche
8. temprano
9. tarde

Vertical

1. ¿Qué hora es?
2. por la tarde
3. a tiempo
4. en punto
7. todo el tiempo

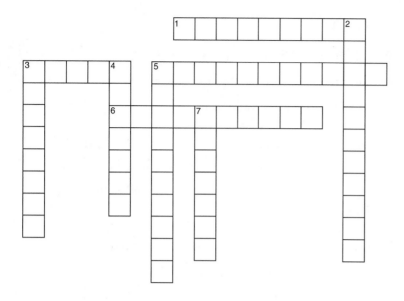

Horizontal

1. What time is it?
3. late
5. in the morning
6. at night

Vertical

2. It's five o'clock.
3. early
4. exactly
5. in the afternoon
7. on time

OPCIONES MÚLTIPLES

Marque con un círculo la letra de la respuesta correcta.

1. **all the time**
   a. todo el tiempo
   b. en punto
   c. tarde
   d. temprano

2. **It's 7:00.**
   a. A las seis.
   b. Son las seis.
   c. Son las siete.
   d. A las siete.

3. **It's 8:00.**
   a. Son las dos.
   b. Son las ocho.
   c. A las dos.
   d. A las ocho.

4. **At 9:00**
   a. Son las nueve y diez.
   b. A las nueve y doce.
   c. Son las nueve y once.
   d. A las nueve.

5. **At 6:30**
   a. Son las siete y media.
   b. A las seis y media.
   c. Son las seis y media.
   d. A las siete y media.

6. **What time is it?**
   a. ¿Qué hora es?
   b. ¿A qué hora?
   c. ¿Cómo estás?
   d. ¿Qué tal?

7. **It's 3:00.**
   a. Son las cinco.
   b. Son las tres.
   c. Son las tres y media.
   d. Son las dos.

8. **exactly, sharp**
   a. tarde
   b. de nada
   c. temprano
   d. en punto

9. **It's 1:00.**
   a. Es la una.
   b. Son las once.
   c. A las once.
   d. A la una.

10. **late**
    a. temprano
    b. tarde
    c. tiempo
    d. ahora

EJERCICIO DE ROLE PLAY

A. **¿ Qué hora es?** Trabaje con un compañero. Pregunte y responda: *What time is it?* Sigue el modelo.

	STUDENT A:	What time is it?
	STUDENT B:	It's three thirty.

1. 2:00
2. 5:00
3. 7:00
4. 11:00

5. 9:30
6. 8:30
7. 4:30
8. 11:30

9. 7:45
10. 5:45
11. 3:45
12. 6:45

B. **¿A qué hora es. . .?** Imagínase que es el primer día de clases. Pregunte y responda a qué hora son las clases. Sigue el modelo.

8:00 History
9:30 Spanish
11:15 English
1:10 Art
2:55 Communication
4:30 Mathematics

STUDENT A:	At what time is History class?
STUDENT B:	At eight o'clock.

1. 8:00   History
2. 9:30   Spanish
3. 11:15   English

4. 1:10   Art
5. 2:55   Communication
6. 4:30   Mathematics

EJERCICIO DE TRADUCCIÓN

Traduzca al español.

1. There are seven days in a week. _____
2. There are four weeks in a month. _____
3. There are four seasons in a year. _____
4. When is your birthday? _____
5. My birthday is May 24. _____
6. Go to Woodland Place on Monday, Tuesday, and Wednesday. _____
7. Go to Maple Apartments on Tuesday and Thursday. _____
8. Go to Oakdale on Monday, Wednesday, and Friday. _____
9. First, go to Old Orchard. _____
10. Second, go to Hoffman Estates. _____
11. What time is it? _____
12. It's 2:00. It's 5:30. _____
13. At what time is the party (la fiesta)? _____
14. The party is at 7:30. _____
15. The party is on Saturday! _____

REPASO

Traduzca al español.

1. How's it going? _____
2. How are you? _____
3. Welcome. _____
4. How's your family? _____
5. What's your name? _____
6. See you later. _____
7. I'd like to introduce you to _____
8. Where are you from? _____
9. Do you speak English? _____
10. Come with me. _____
11. Watch me. _____
12. Do it like me. _____
13. Help me. _____
14. It's important. _____
15. You're a hard worker! _____

Lea el diálogo en voz alta en inglés.	*Lea el diálogo en voz alta en español.*
Seguidamente tradúzcalo al español.	*Seguidamente tradúzcalo al inglés.*

Welcome!	Party!
What:	A Celebration!
When:	Saturday, March 3
	At 6:00 pm
Where:	1620 Highland
Who:	Mark
Office:	770-845-6293
Cell:	770-292-5856

¡Bienvenidos!	¡Una Fiesta!
Qué:	¡Una Celebración!
Cuándo:	sábado, 3 de marzo
	a las seis de la noche
Dónde:	1620 Highland
Quién:	Mark
Oficina:	770-845-6293
Cell:	770-292-5856

Gloria: There is a party!

Pablo: Fantastic! When is it?

Gloria: On Saturday... March 3.

Pablo: Where is the party?

Gloria: 5600 Sherman Avenue.

Pablo: At what time?

Gloria: At 6:00.

(on Saturday at the party ... there is a lot of music ...)

Mark: Hello. Welcome!

Gloria: Thank you.

Pablo: How's it going?

Mark: Magnificent!

Mark: I want to introduce you to Octavio.

Gloria: Nice to meet you.

Octavio: Same to you.

Gloria: Where are you from, Octavio?

Octavio: I'm from Oaxaca. I'm Mexican.

Gloria: Do you speak English?

Octavio: Yes. Do you speak English, Gloria?

Gloria: I'm studying English.

Mark: I'm studying Spanish.

Octavio: Perfect! Where is the beer?

(she directs them to the kitchen)

Gloria: Incredible!

Pablo: There is pizza and salad.

Gloria: Yes... And there are many tacos and burritos!

Octavio: First... A beer!

Gloria: ¡Hay una fiesta!

Pablo: ¡Fantástico! ¿Cuándo es?

Gloria: El sábado... el 3 de marzo.

Pablo: ¿Dónde está la fiesta?

Gloria: 5600 Sherman Avenue.

Pablo: ¿A qué hora?

Gloria: A las seis.

(el sábado a la fiesta... hay mucha música...)

Mark: Hola. ¡Bienvenidos!

Gloria: Gracias.

Pablo: ¿Qué tal?

Mark: ¡Magnífico!

Mark: Quiero presentarte a Octavio.

Gloria: Mucho gusto.

Octavio: Igualmente.

Gloria: ¿De dónde eres, Octavio?

Octavio: Soy de Oaxaca. Soy mejicano.

Gloria: ¿Hablas inglés?

Octavio: Si. ¿Hablas inglés, Gloria?

Gloria: Estudio inglés.

Mark: Estudio español.

Octavio: ¡Perfecto! ¿Dónde está la cerveza?

(los dirige a la cocina)

Gloria: ¡Increíble!

Pablo: Hay pizza y ensalada.

Gloria: Sí... ¡Y hay muchos tacos y burritos!

Octavio: Primero... ¡Una cerveza!

LA CULTURA: EL MANEJO DEL TIEMPO

Cuando estadounidenses y latinoamericanos trabajan juntos, una de las mayores dificultades que se presentan, además de la barrera del idioma, es el diferente sentido del tiempo. Cada cultura trata al tiempo de manera muy particular. Se debe comprender que para los empleados que vienen de otro país en el cual el tiempo se ve y se administra de otra manera, el sentido del tiempo de los estadounidenses es uno de los aspectos más difíciles para su adaptación.

Puesto que "el tiempo es oro" en los Estados Unidos y puesto que el dinero es el factor principal de los negocios, todas las decisiones, todas las actividades, todos los compromisos, bien sea en el trabajo o en el hogar, de los estadounidenses están controlados por el reloj. El empleado siempre está bajo presión para cumplir sus compromisos a tiempo. Se considera que la falta de puntualidad es casi una desgracia. Los negocios y los placeres se miden con el reloj. Se afirma a menudo que los estadounidenses son "esclavos de nada, excepto del reloj."

Para la gente en los Estados Unidos, tiene gran importancia llegar a cada reunión exactamente a la hora acordada. La puntualidad se equipara con la confiabilidad y la eficacia, que son valores significativos en la cultura estadounidense, mientras que las faltas de puntualidad y los retrasos sugieren lo contrario.

Muchos latinos viven sin regirse por un calendario ni un reloj. La idea estadounidense de usar una agenda para planificar todas las actividades del día en bloques horarios exactos sigue siendo extraña para muchos latinos. Según su punto de vista, ésto no permitiría el curso natural de las cosas.

Mientras que un ciudadano estadounidense que haga una cola en un supermercado podría estar extremadamente consciente de tener que esperar cuatro o cinco minutos para que le atiendan, un latino se pasaría ese rato hablando con un amigo o simplemente esperando con paciencia y cortesía. Desde la perspectiva de un latino, los impacientes ciudadanos estadounidenses pueden parecer descorteses, bruscos o incluso detestables. En una sociedad que valora la cortesía por encima de la eficacia, las manifestaciones abiertas de impaciencia parecen contraproducentes en muchas ocasiones.

El sentimiento de relajación respecto al tiempo está comenzando a cambiar entre los profesionales latinos modernos. A medida que la gente latina lleva vidas más complejas y aumentan las presiones para lograr una mayor productividad, los latinos comienzan a preocuparse más por la puntualidad y cumplir más con las citas acordadas. Pero se trata de un proceso gradual y la opinión general entre los latinos sigue siendo que "*lo que no hagamos hoy lo haremos mañana.*" Esos niveles extremos de conciencia de la importancia del tiempo que tienen los estadounidenses no se compaginan naturalmente con la forma de pensar de la mayoría de los latinos, quienes prefieren tomarse la vida en forma más relajada.

CAPITULO
4

La Familia y El Personal del Trabajo

PARTE I   LA FAMILIA

la familia
family

los abuelos
grandparents

los padres
parents

la madre
mother

el padre
father

el hijo
son

la hija
daughter

los hijos
children

el hermano
brother

la hermana
sister

la esposa
wife

el esposo
husband

la tía
aunt

el tío
uncle

el primo/la prima
cousin

41

LA GRAMÁTICA: "THE"

En inglés "the" es la única forma para expresar las palabras: el, la, los, y las.

los tacos	**the tacos**
la salsa	**the salsa**
los burritos	**the burritos**
las cervezas	**the beers**
los amigos	**the friends**
las fiestas	**the parties**
el patio	**the patio**
la Margarita	**the Margarita**

EJERCICIO DE CORRESPONDENCIA

Escriba la letra de cada dibujo al lado de la palabra inglesa que corresponde abajo.

a.

b.

c.

d.

e.

f.

g.

h.

i.

j.

k.

l.

1. _____ aunt
2. _____ cousin
3. _____ family
4. _____ children
5. _____ sister
6. _____ uncle
7. _____ son
8. _____ grandparents
9. _____ mother
10. _____ wife
11. _____ father
12. _____ brother

EJERCICIO DE VOCABULARIO

Escriba la palabra inglesa abajo.

1. _____

2. _____

3. _____

4. _____

5. _____

6. _____

7. _____

8. _____

9. _____

EJERCICIO DE CORRESPONDENCIA

Escriba la letra de la palabra en español junto a la palabra inglesa que corresponda a la izquierda.

1. _____ family
2. _____ brother
3. _____ cousins
4. _____ wife
5. _____ aunt

6. _____ husband
7. _____ grandparents
8. _____ uncle
9. _____ mother
10. _____ father

a. familia
b. primos
c. hermano
d. tía
e. tío

f. abuelos
g. esposa
h. padre
i. madre
j. esposo

CRUCIGRAMAS

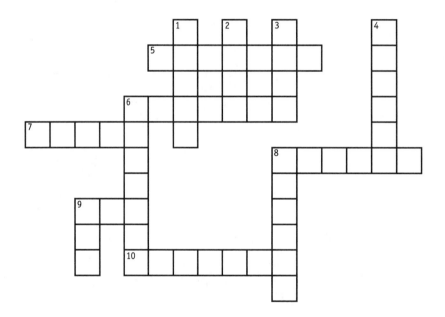

Horizontal

5. family
6. brother
7. father
8. wife
9. aunt
10. grandparents

Vertical

1. mother
2. daughter
3. son
4. parents
6. sister
8. husband
9. uncle

Horizontal

1. esposo
3. hija
5. hijo
6. tía
7. esposa
8. primo
10. madre

Vertical

2. hermano
4. abuelos
9. tío

EJERCICIO DE TRADUCCIÓN

Traduzca al inglés.

1. el hermano _____
2. la madre _____
3. el primo _____
4. el tío _____
5. la familia _____
6. la hermana _____
7. el esposo _____
8. el padre _____
9. el hijo _____
10. los abuelos _____

Traduzca al español.

1. wife _____
2. sister _____
3. grandparents _____
4. family _____
5. brother _____
6. aunt _____
7. cousin _____
8. mother _____
9. father _____
10. daughter _____

OPCIONES MÚLTIPLES

Marque con un círculo la letra de la respuesta correcta.

1. **father**
   a. hermano
   b. primo
   c. madre
   d. padre

2. **husband**
   a. hermano
   b. esposo
   c. hijo
   d. tío

3. **cousin**
   a. hermano
   b. primo
   c. madre
   d. padre

4. **mother**
   a. madre
   b. tía
   c. hermana
   d. hija

5. **grandparents**
   a. hermanos
   b. primos
   c. abuelos
   d. hijos

6. **aunt**
   a. hija
   b. madre
   c. hermana
   d. tía

7. **family**
   a. abuelos
   b. primos
   c. familia
   d. madre

8. **brother**
   a. hermano
   b. primo
   c. madre
   d. padre

9. **son**
   a. hija
   b. hijo
   c. hermano
   d. hermana

10. **wife**
    a. hija
    b. tía
    c. hermana
    d. esposa

EJERCICIO DE ROLE PLAY

A. **¿Cómo se llama?** En el Capítulo 1, usted aprendió cómo preguntarle a sus compañeros de trabajo sus nombres y a decir el suyo. Ahora, trabajando con un compañero, pregúntele los nombres de los miembros de su familia en la foto. "My" significa "mi." "Your" significa "tu." Sigue el modelo.

(hijo / Raul)

STUDENT A: What's your son's name?
STUDENT B: My son's name is Raúl.

1. madre / Margarita
2. hermano / Guillermo
3. hija / Raquel
4. hermana / Cristina
5. hijo / Raúl
6. tío / Samuel
7. padre / Ignacio
8. abuelo / Ricardo

B. **¿Cuántos años tiene?** Trabaje con un compañero. Pregunte y responda: *How old is. . .?* Sigue el modelo.

(Raúl, 6)

STUDENT A:	How old is Raúl?
STUDENT B:	Raul is six years old.

1. Margarita, 43   5. Raúl, 6
2. Guillermo, 18   6. Samuel, 39
3. Raquel, 8   7. Ignacio, 55
4. Cristina, 22   8. Ricardo, 69

C. **¿Cuántos años tienes?** Pregunte y responda: *How old are you? I am _____ years old.* Sigue el modelo.

(Adam, 20)

STUDENT A:	How old are you, Adam?
STUDENT B:	I'm twenty years old.

1. Marta, 18   5. Nancy, 50
2. Rodolfo, 72   6. Gustavo, 61
3. Bob, 34   7. Enrique, 83
4. Frank, 45   8. Sonia, 29

PARTE II   EL PERSONAL DEL TRABAJO

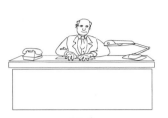

el jefe
boss

la secretaria
secretary

el mayordomo
foreman, crew leader

la cuadrilla
crew

los amigos
friends

el mecánico
technician

el (la) gerente
manager

el (la) cliente
customer

la mujer
woman

el hombre
man

el vecino
neighbor

EJERCICIO DE CORRESPONDENCIA

Escriba la letra de cada dibujo al lado de la palabra inglesa que corresponde abajo.

a.

b.

c.

d.   e.

f.

g.

h.

i.

j.

1. _____ boss

2. _____ manager

3. _____ customer

4. _____ woman

5. _____ technician

6. _____ secretary

7. _____ foreman, crew leader

8. _____ crew

9. _____ friends

10. _____ neighbor

EJERCICIO DE VOCABULARIO

Escriba la palabra inglesa abajo.

1. _____

2. _____

3. _____

4. _____

5. _____

6. _____

7. _____

8. _____

EJERCICIO DE CORRESPONDENCIA

Escriba la letra de la palabra en español junto a la palabra inglesa que corresponda a la izquierda.

1. _____ technician   a. mecánico
2. _____ secretary   b. mayordomo
3. _____ man   c. jefe
4. _____ boss   d. gerente
5. _____ neighbor   e. secretaria
6. _____ friend   f. amigo
7. _____ manager   g. cliente
8. _____ woman   h. mujer
9. _____ customer   i. hombre
10. _____ foreman   j. vecino
11. _____ crew   k. cuadrilla

CRUCIGRAMAS

Horizontal

5. secretary
6. manager
7. neighbor
9. foreman, crew leader

Vertical

1. crew
2. friends
3. boss
4. woman
8. man

Horizontal

3. vecino
7. secretaria
8. mujer
9. hombre
10. mecánico

Vertical

1. jefe
2. amigos
4. cuadrilla
5. mayordomo
6. gerente

EJERCICIO DE TRADUCCIÓN

Traduzca al inglés.

1. la secretaria _____
2. el mecánico _____
3. el jefe _____
4. el mayordomo _____
5. el gerente _____
6. la mujer _____
7. el cuadrilla _____
8. el hombre _____
9. el amigo _____
10. el (la) cliente _____

Traduzca al español.

1. crew _____
2. foreman _____
3. boss _____
4. friend _____
5. woman _____
6. customer _____
7. technician _____
8. secretary _____
9. manager _____
10. man _____

OPCIONES MÚLTIPLES

Marque con un círculo la letra de la respuesta correcta.

1. **woman**
   a. jefe
   b. hombre
   c. mujer
   d. secretaria

2. **crew leader**
   a. mayordomo
   b. jefe
   c. vecino
   d. hombre

3. **friends**
   a. mujer
   b. hombre
   c. cuadrilla
   d. amigos

4. **man**
   a. jefe
   b. hombre
   c. mujer
   d. vecino

5. **neighbor**
   a. mayordomo
   b. jefe
   c. vecino
   d. hombre

6. **boss**
   a. mayordomo
   b. jefe
   c. vecino
   d. hombre

7. **crew**
   a. mujer
   b. hombre
   c. cuadrilla
   d. amigos

8. **manager**
   a. gerente
   b. jefe
   c. mayordomo
   d. mujer

9. **technician**
   a. mayordomo
   b. mujer
   c. hombre
   d. mecánico

10. **secretary**
    a. jefe
    b. hombre
    c. mujer
    d. secretaria

PARTE III   LOS TIPOS DE PERSONALIDAD Y LAS EMOCIONES

Cognados son palabras que son muy parecidas en los dos idiomas. Los siguientes cognados describen personas.

agresivo, a	**aggressive**	intelectual	**intellectual**
ambicioso, a	**ambitious**	inteligente	**intelligent**
cómico, a	**comical**	introvertido, a	**introverted**
cooperativo, a	**cooperative**	materialista	**materialistic**
cruel	**cruel**	organizado, a	**organized**
extrovertido, a	**extroverted**	paciente	**patient**
generoso, a	**generous**	responsable	**responsible**
justo, a	**fair**	romántico, a	**romantic**
trabajador / trabajadora	**hardworking**	sencible	**sensitive**
honesto, a	**honest**	sincero, a	**sincere**
impaciente	**impatient**	sociable	**sociable**
impulsivo, a	**impulsive**	supersticioso, a	**superstitious**
independiente	**independent**	tímido, a	**timid**

EJERCICIO DE VOCABULARIO

A. Escriba sus initiales al lado de las caracteristicas que usted tiene.

agresivo, a _____   intelectual _____

ambicioso, a _____   inteligente _____

cómico, a _____   introvertido, a _____

cooperativo, a _____   materialista _____

cruel _____   organizado, a _____

extrovertido, a _____   paciente _____

generoso, a _____   responsable _____

justo, a _____   romántico, a _____

trabajador-dora _____   sencible _____

honesto,a _____   sincero, a _____

impaciente _____   sociable _____

impulsivo, a _____   supersticioso, a _____

independiente _____   tímido, a _____

B. Ahora, escriba las iniciales de uno de sus compañeros o una persona con quien trabaja.

C. Ahora, escriba las iniciales de su esposo/a o novio/a.

LA GRAMÁTICA: "SER" Y "TO BE"

Ser	to be
Soy	I am
Eres	You are
Es	He, she is

1. El verbo "to be" significa "ser."

Soy de California.   **I am from California.**

¿De dónde eres?   **Where are you from?**

Juan es de Honduras.   **Juan is from Honduras.**

2. También usamos "to be" para describir una persona.

Soy cómica.   **I am comical.**

Eres ambicioso.   **You are ambitious.**

María es inteligente.   **María is intelligent.**

CUÁNTO

muy	**very**
no muy	**not very**
un poco	**a little**
un poquito	**a very little**

EJERCICIOS

A. Use las palabras inglesas de la lista de cognados y escoja las de la lista para describirse.

Responda con lo siguiente: 1) un cognado que es muy característico de usted, 2) un cognado que no es tan característico de usted 3) un cognado que no es característico de usted.

1. I am very _____

2. I am a little _____

3. I am not very _____

B. Ahora, describa uno de sus compañeros o una persona con quien trabaja.

1. is very _____

2. is a little _____

3. is not very _____

C. Para cumplir cada frase, ponga un cognado en la línea. Cada frase empieza con "Usted es"/"Tu eres."

1. You are very _____

2. You are a little _____

3. You are not very _____

D. Imagínese que usted está escribiendo un anuncio de requerimiento. Haga una lista de las características que usted necesita y que debe tener un empleado.

_____

_____

_____

_____

E. Ponga en cada línea uno de los cognados/una de las características.

1. The technician is _____

2. My friend is _____

3. My boss is _____

4. The manager is _____

5. The secretary is _____

6. The foreman is _____

7. The man is _____

8. The customer is _____

9. The neighbor is _____

10. The woman is _____

LAS EMOCIONES

¿Cómo estás?	**How are you?**	ocupado, a	**busy**
Estoy. . .	**I am. . .**	preocupado, a	**worried**
		triste	**sad**
cansado, a	**tired**	feliz	**happy**
confundido, a	**confused**	enfermo, a	**sick**
contento, a	**content**	de buen humor	**good mood**
enojado, a	**angry**	de mal humor	**bad mood**
furioso, a	**furious**		
nervioso, a	**nervous**		

EJERCICIO DE CORRESPONDENCIA

Escriba la letra de la palabra en español junto a la palabra inglesa que corresponda a la izquierda.

1. _____ good mood
2. _____ content
3. _____ happy
4. _____ sick
5. _____ tired
6. _____ sad
7. _____ angry
8. _____ busy

9. _____ worried
10. _____ bad mood
11. _____ furious
12. _____ nervous
13. _____ confused
14 _____ How are you?
15. _____ I am. . .

a. Estoy. . .
b. preocupado, a
c. triste
d. ¿Cómo estás?
e. feliz
f. de buen humor
g. de mal humor
h. confundido, a

i. contento, a
j. cansado, a
k. enojado, a
l. nervioso, a
m. furioso, a
n. enfermo, a
o. ocupado, a

CRUCIGRAMAS

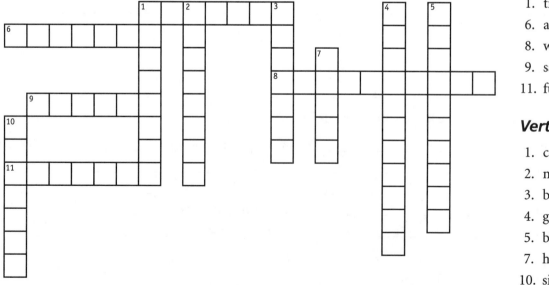

Horizontal

1. tired
6. angry
8. worried
9. sad
11. furious

Vertical

1. content
2. nervous
3. busy
4. good mood
5. bad mood
7. happy
10. sick

Horizontal

2. nervioso
5. de mal humor
6. enfermo
8. enojado
11. cansado
12. ocupado

Vertical

1. de buen humor
3. feliz
4. preocupado
7. contento
9. furioso
10. triste

LA GRAMÁTICA: "ESTAR" Y LAS EMOCIONES

Estar	**To be**
Estoy	**I am**
Estás	**You are**
Está	**He is, she is**

Como usted sabe, cuando queremos preguntarle a alguien cómo se siente, decimos "*How are you?*" (*¿Cómo estás?*). Cuando queremos decir cómo se siente alguien usamos también el verbo "*to be*" ("*ser*").

Estoy preocupado.	**I am worried.**
¿Estás nervioso?	**Are you nervous?**
¡La cliente está enojada!	**The client is angry!**

EJERCICIO DE TRADUCCIÓN

Traduzca al inglés.

1. Estoy enfermo. _____

2. ¿Estás preocupado? _____

3. ¿Está enojado? _____

4. Estoy triste. _____

5. ¡Está furiosa! _____

6. Está ocupada. _____

7. ¿Estás de mal humor? _____

8. Estoy confundido. _____

9. Estoy cansado. _____

10. ¿Está feliz? _____

11. ¡Estás de buen humor! _____

12. ¿Estás contenta? _____

Traduzca al español.

1. Are you sick? _____

2. Is she angry? _____

3. I am worried. _____

4. Are you confused? _____

5. You're in a good mood! _____

6. I am fine. _____

7. Are you busy? _____

8. He is happy. _____

9. Are you tired? _____

10. He is in a bad mood. _____

11. She is furious! _____

12. I am nervous. _____

OPCIONES MÚLTIPLES

Marque con un círculo la letra de la respuesta correcta.

1. Are you sick?
   a. Está triste.
   b. ¿Estás enfermo?
   c. Está mal.
   d. Estás bien.

2. She is in a good mood.
   a. Está bien.
   b. Está de buen humor.
   c. Está contenta.
   d. Estoy contenta.

3. Is he angry?
   a. ¿Estás enojado?
   b. ¿Estás cansado?
   c. ¿Está enojado?
   d. ¿Estoy enojado?

4. Are you sad?
   a. ¿Estás triste?
   b. ¿Estás enojado?
   c. ¿Estás mal?
   d. ¿Estás enfermo?

5. I am worried.
   a. Estoy preocupado.
   b. Estoy ocupado.
   c. Estoy enojado.
   d. Estoy tiste.

6. He is in a bad mood.
   a. Está enojado.
   b. Estoy mal.
   c. Estoy enojado.
   d. Está de mal humor.

7. Are you tired?
   a. ¿Estás contento?
   b. Estoy cansado.
   c. ¿Estás cansado?
   d. ¿Estás confundido?

8. Are you nervous?
   a. ¿Estás nervioso?
   b. Estoy nervioso.
   c. Está enojado.
   d. ¿Estás enojado?

9. She is furious!
   a. ¡Está furioso!
   b. ¡Está furiosa!
   c. ¡Estoy furiosa!
   d. ¡Estoy furioso!

10. Are you confused?
   a. Estoy cansada.
   b. Estoy confundida.
   c. ¿Estás confundida?
   d. ¿Estás contenta?

EJERCICIO DE TRADUCCIÓN

Traduzca al español.

1. There are five children in my family. _____

2. There are four brothers. _____

3. What's your uncle's name? _____

4. What's your son's name? _____

5. How old is your daughter? _____

6. Christina is five years old. _____

7. My son is responsible and cooperative. _____

8. My manager is comical and organized. _____

9. The crew is hardworking. _____

10. The client is furious! _____

11. Are there problems? _____

12. I am nervous and worried. _____

13. My boss is angry! _____

14. The supervisor is in a good mood. _____

15. Are you sick? Sad? Confused? _____

REPASO

Lea el cuento en voz alta en inglés. Seguidamente tradúzcalo al español.

Hello. My name is Octavio. I'm from Oaxaca, Mexico. I'm Mexican. I'm twenty-two years old. There are twelve people in my family. I have four brothers, two sisters, my parents and my four grandparents. I am sad because* my family is in Mexico and I am in the United States. I speak Spanish. . .I don't speak English.

*because – porque

    In the United States I have many good friends. I have many good girlfriends. Gloria is the woman that interests* me!

    Gloria works** at White's Nursery. Gloria is generous, sincere, comical, and very romantic. She is nineteen years old. She is from Guanajato, Mexico. She is intelligent. Gloria speaks a little English.

  *interests me – me interesa
**works – trabaja

    Gloria's family is large. Gloria has three brothers in the United States. Her brother is the foreman of my crew. His name is Manuel. Manuel is twenty five years old and is very responsible, organized and fair. Manuel speaks English and Spanish. He is bilingual. Her brother, Luis, is twenty three years old and is cooperative, hard working, and very sensitive. Luis is on my crew. Her brother, Raimundo, is the mechanic. Raimundo is comical and always in a good mood.

Lea el cuento en voz alta en español. Seguidamente tradúzcalo al inglés.

Hola. Me llamo Octavio. Soy de Oaxaca, Mejico. Soy mejicano. Tengo 22 años. Hay doce personas en mi familia. Tengo cuatro hermanos, dos hermanas, mis padres y cuatro abuelos. Estoy triste porque* mi familia está en Mejico y estoy in los Estados Unidos. Hablo español. . .no hablo inglés.

*porque – because

En los Estados Unidos tengo muchos amigos buenos. Tengo muchas buenas amigas. ¡Gloria es la mujer que me interesa*!

Gloria trabaja** en White's Nursery. Gloria es generosa, sincera, cómica y muy romántica. Tiene 19 años. Es de Guanajato, Mexico. Es inteligente. Gloria habla inglés un poco.

*me interesa – interests me
**trabaja – works

La familia de Gloria es grande. Gloria tiene tres hermanos en los Estados Unidos. Su hermano es el mayordomo de mi cuadrilla. Se llama Manuel. Manuel tiene 25 años y es muy responsible, organizado y justo. Manuel habla inglés y español. Es bilingue. Su hermano, Luis, tiene 23 años y es cooperativo, trabajador, y muy frágil. Luis es en mi cuadrillo. Su hermano, Raimundo, es el mecánico. Raimundo es cómico y siempre está de buen humor.

Traduzca al español.

1. Monday, Wednesday, Friday _____

2. Tuesday, Thursday, Saturday _____

3. March, June, August _____

4. January, December, September _____

5. There is salad, pizza, and beer. _____

6. Is there music? _____

7. What's your name? _____

8. Where are you from? _____

9. I'd like to introduce you to _____

10. How are you? _____

11. Come with me. _____

12. Do it like me. _____

13. Try it. Keep trying. _____

14. You're a hard worker! _____

15. Good work! _____

16. It's important. It's necessary. _____

17. It's good. It's bad. It's so-so. _____

18. Everything else is perfect. _____

19. Where is the manager? _____

20. How many? _____

LA CULTURA: LA FAMILIA

Una expresión común en español es "*La familia sobre todo*," resaltando el gran valor que le atribuyen los latinos a su familia. Obviamente esto significa que "la familia está por encima de todo lo demás." La familia es la principal prioridad, antes que el trabajo y todos los otros aspectos de la vida.

La fortaleza de la sociedad latina sigue siendo la unidad familiar tradicional. A esta familia latina se le denomina a menudo "*el clan familiar*" puesto que incluye no sólo a los padres y sus hijos, sino también a tías, tíos, primos y abuelos.

Dentro de la familia tradicional, el padre es la autoridad indisputable, así como el encargado de mantener la disciplina. Todas las decisiones esenciales son tomadas por él. Tradicionalmente, la madre asume un papel subordinado en la familia latina y busca los consejos y la autoridad de su esposo para todas las cuestiones de importancia. Se presume que es una madre devota y abnegada y es sumamente valorada por serlo. Los padres se dedican a sus hijos. Los hijos son protegidos y mimados, y el típico entretenimiento de los fines de semana consiste en la reunión de toda la familia, incluyendo abuelos, tías, tíos y primos. Al ser criados en estas circunstancias, los niños se sienten protegidos, pero también se acostumbran a depender mucho de la ayuda de sus familias.

Al comenzar la escuela, normalmente los niños latinos están de acuerdo con lo que piensan los demás, es decir, sus maestros, aceptando la inflexibilidad del sistema escolar. Los niños latinos creen que sus maestros son la autoridad indisputable y suprimen todo deseo de cuestionamiento de esa autoridad en su mente. Debido a esta crianza y educación, al llegar a un lugar de trabajo, los jóvenes empleados latinos aceptan las instrucciones sin cuestionarlas y les parecen sumisos a sus supervisores. Al pensar que su supervisor tiene una autoridad absoluta, la responsabilidad del subordinado se limita a llevar a cabo el trabajo que le asigna su jefe.

La palabra "familia" en los Estados Unidos se refiere tradicionalmente sólo a los padres y sus hijos. En una típica familia estadounidense, la madre y el padre se consideran personas con el mismo nivel de autoridad.

En los Estados Unidos, a menudo se le da mayor importancia al trabajo que a la familia. Se presume que la familia encajará de alguna manera entre los horarios y las actividades del trabajo. También se espera que los empleados se muden con toda su familia si consiguen un ascenso en el trabajo. No es raro ver que las familias se mudan muchas veces durante el desarrollo de la carrera profesional de sus miembros. Así, las familias se dispersan y viven en muchos lugares diferentes de los Estados Unidos. A menudo los padres y los hermanos sólo se ven en raras ocasiones cada año.

Los divorcios son algo común. El estado actual de la familia y la pérdida de los valores familiares tradicionales (por ejemplo, las cenas en familia cocinadas y compartidas en el hogar cada noche) han causado gran controversia durante muchos años. Las situaciones creadas por estas razones han colocado cargas adicionales sobre el padre o la madre que cría a sus hijos sin la ayuda de su esposa o esposo, puesto que ahora esa madre o padre solitario tiene menos tiempo disponible para los niños debido a la necesidad de trabajar a tiempo completo fuera del hogar.

Un niño criado en este tipo de familia o en un hogar donde ambos padres trabajen a tiempo completo tiene que realizar muchas tareas por su cuenta. Ese niño es responsable por muchas cosas desde muy pequeño. Al crecer, este niño llega a ser una persona autónoma, independiente e individualista; características que son consideradas positivas en los Estados Unidos. Debido a esta crianza, los jóvenes llegan a una organización comercial o empresa llenos de confianza en sí mismos. Tienen muchas de las características que se admiran en un empleado. Piensan con independencia e ideas propias y son dinámicos y competitivos. Se sienten a gusto intercambiando opiniones con sus supervisores, así como asumiendo cargos de responsabilidad.

5

Los Deportes y Las Actividades

PARTE I   LOS DEPORTES

jugar al béisbol
to play baseball

jugar al básquetbol
to play basketball

jugar al fútbol americano
to play football

jugar al fútbol
to play soccer

jugar al tenis
to play tennis

jugar al golf
to play golf

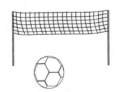

jugar al volibol
to play volleyball

jugar a los deportes
to play sports

jugar al boliche
to bowl

jugar al billar
to play billiards

pescar
to fish

nadar
to swim

EJERCICIO DE VOCABULARIO

Escriba la palabra inglesa abajo.

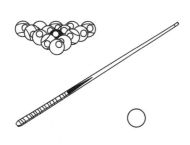

1. _____

2. _____

3. _____

4. _____

5. _____

6. _____

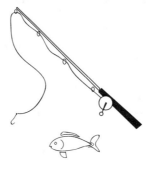

7. _____

8. _____

9. _____

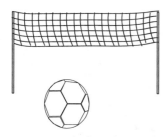

10. _____

11. _____

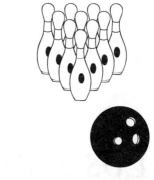

12. _____

EJERCICIO DE CORRESPONDENCIA

Escriba la letra de la palabra en español junto a la palabra inglesa que corresponda a la izquierda.

1. _____ to play basketball   a. jugar al volibol
2. _____ to bowl   b. jugar a los deportes
3. _____ to fish   c. jugar al fútbol
4. _____ to play baseball   d. pescar
5. _____ to swim   e. jugar al boliche
6. _____ to play sports   f. jugar al básquetbol
7. _____ to play golf   g. jugar al béisbol
8. _____ to play volleyball   h. jugar al golf
9. _____ to play billiards   i. nadar
10. _____ to play soccer   j. jugar al billar

CRUCIGRAMAS

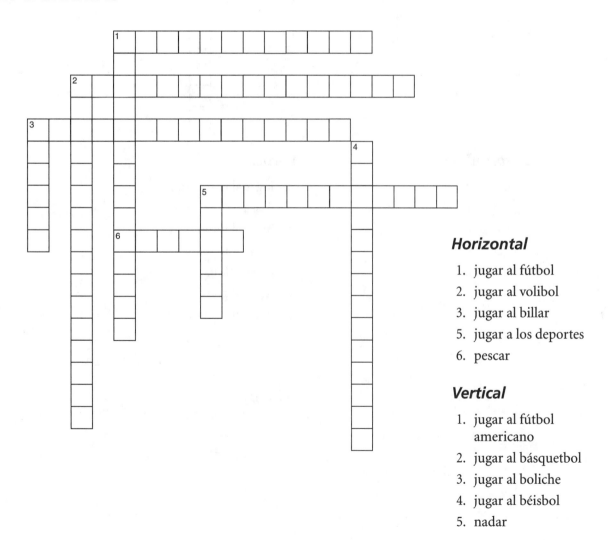

Horizontal

1. jugar al fútbol
2. jugar al volibol
3. jugar al billar
5. jugar a los deportes
6. pescar

Vertical

1. jugar al fútbol americano
2. jugar al básquetbol
3. jugar al boliche
4. jugar al béisbol
5. nadar

Horizontal

1. nadar
4. jugar al fútbol americano
6. jugar al tenis
8. jugar al boliche
9. jugar a los deportes

Vertical

1. jugar al básquetbol
2. pescar
3. jugar al fútbol
4. jugar al beísbol
5. jugar al billar
6. jugar al golf
7. jugar al volibol

EJERCICIO DE TRADUCCIÓN

Traduzca al español.

1. to play golf _____

2. to play sports _____

3. to play billiards _____

4. to play soccer _____

5. to swim _____

6. to fish _____

7. to bowl _____

8. to play volleyball _____

9. to play basketball _____

10. to play tennis _____

LA GRAMÁTICA: GUSTOS

Para expresar gustos, use las palabras "Do you like. . .?" Estudie los siguientes ejemplos:

¿Te gusta jugar al fútbol?   **Do you like to play soccer?**

¿Te gusta jugar al béisbol?   **Do you like to play baseball?**

¿Te gusta jugar al golf?   **Do you like to play golf?**

Sí, me gusta ir a las fiestas.   **Yes, I like to go to parties.**

No, no me gusta ir a las fiestas.   **No, I do not like to go to parties.**

EJERCICIO DE TRADUCCIÓN

Traduzca al inglés.

1. ¿Te gusta jugar al volibol? _____

2. ¿Te gusta pescar? _____

3. ¿Te gusta nadar? _____

4. ¿Te gusta jugar a los deportes? _____

5. ¿Te gusta jugar al golf? _____

Traduzca al español.

1. Do you like to play volleyball? _____

2. Do you like to swim? _____

3. Do you like to play tennis? _____

4. Do you like fish? _____

5. Do you like to play sports? _____

6. Do you like to play basketball? _____

7. Do you like to play baseball? _____

8. Do you like to play soccer? _____

9. Do you like to play billiards? _____

10. Do you like to bowl? _____

EJERCICIO DE ROLE PLAY

A. **Me gusta o me encanta (*I like to* o también *I love to*). . .** imagínese que usted está trabajando en un campus universitario con canchas deportivas. Indique si a usted le encanta (*love. . .* me encanta), le gusta (*like. . .* me gusta) o no le gusta (*don't like. . .* no me gusta) practicar el deporte indicado. Use una de las siguientes frases.

Me encanta jugar al fútbol.   **I love to play soccer.**
Me gusta jugar al fútbol.   **I like to play soccer.**
No me gusta jugar al fútbol.   **I do not like to play soccer.**

1.

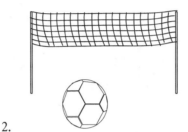

2.

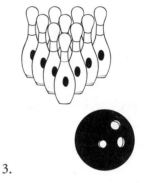

3.

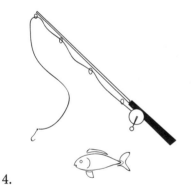

4.

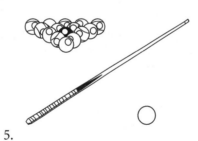

5.

6.

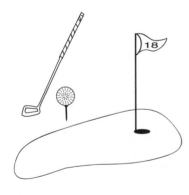

7.

8.

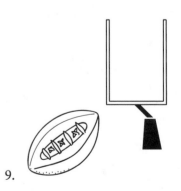

9.

10.

B. **¿Qué le gusta hacer?** Trabajando con un compañero, pregúntele cuales actividades le gustan a él o a ella y cuales actividades no le gustan hacer en cada estación. Sigue el modelo.

STUDENT A: What do you like to do in the Spring?
STUDENT B: I like to play baseball but I don't like to swim.

1.

2.

3.

4.

C. **¿Con quién?** Trabaje con un compañero diciéndose cuándo y con quién les gusta practicar estos deportes. Sigue el modelo.

verano/volibol/amigos   In the summer I like to play volleyball with my friends.

1. beisbol/hermanos 2. fútbol/supervisores   3. nadar/hijos   4. básquetbol/tío

5. fútbol/mecánico   6. pescar/jefe   7. billar/padre   8. boliche/familia

PARTE II   LAS ACTIVIDADES

leer
to read

bailar
to dance

ir a fiestas
to go to parties

estar con la familia
to be with family

jugar a las cartas
to play cards

tomar, beber
to drink

comer
to eat

escuchar la música
to listen to music

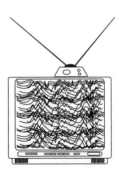

mirar la televisión
to watch television

EJERCICIO DE CORRESPONDENCIA

Escriba la letra de cada dibujo al lado de la palabra inglesa que corresponde abajo.

a.

b.

c.

d.

e.

f.

g.

h.

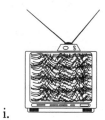

i.

1. _____ to dance
2. _____ to read
3. _____ to eat
4. _____ to drink
5. _____ to go to parties

6. _____ to watch television
7. _____ to listen to music
8. _____ to play cards
9. _____ to be with family

EJERCICIO DE VOCABULARIO

Escriba la palabra inglesa abajo.

1. _____

2. _____

3. _____

4. _____

5. _____

6. _____

7. _____

8. _____

9. _____

EJERCICIO DE CORRESPONDENCIA

Escriba la letra de la palabra en español junto a la palabra inglesa que corresponda a la izquierda.

1. _____ to listen to music   a. tomar, beber
2. _____ to read   b. jugar cartas
3. _____ to dance   c. ir a fiestas
4. _____ to play cards   d. mirar la televisión
5. _____ to be with family   e. leer
6. _____ to watch television   f. estar con la familia
7. _____ to eat   g. escuchar la música
8. _____ to drink   h. comer
9. _____ to go to parties   i. bailar

CRUCIGRAMAS

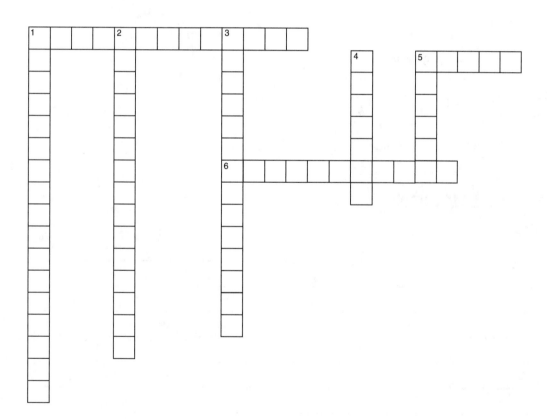

Horizontal

1. ir a fiestas
5. comer
6. jugar cartas

Vertical

1. mirar la televisión
2. escuchar música
3. estar con familia
4. bailar
5. leer

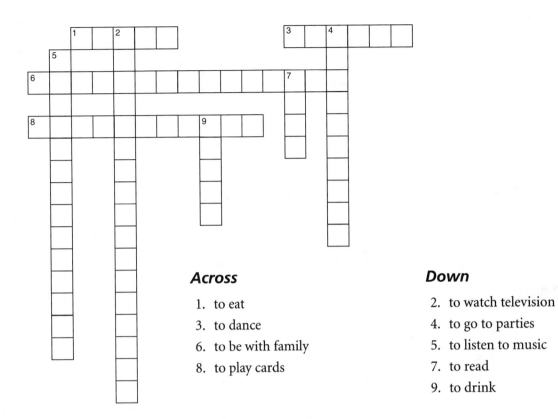

Across

1. to eat
3. to dance
6. to be with family
8. to play cards

Down

2. to watch television
4. to go to parties
5. to listen to music
7. to read
9. to drink

EJERCICIO DE TRADUCCIÓN

Traduzca al inglés.

1. ir a fiestas _____

2. mirar la televisión _____

3. bailar _____

4. estar con la familia _____

5. tomar _____

6. comer _____

7. jugar cartas _____

8. escuchar la música _____

9. leer _____

10. jugar al béisbol _____

Traduzca al español.

1. to listen to music _____

2. to read _____

3. to dance _____

4. to drink _____

5. to eat _____

6. to go to parties _____

7. to watch T.V. _____

8. to be with family _____

9. to play cards _____

10. to play soccer _____

OPCIONES MÚLTIPLES

Marque con un círculo la letra de la respuesta correcta.

1. **to listen to music**
   a. mirar la televisión
   b. escuchar la radio
   c. escuchar la música
   d. ir a fiestas

2. **to dance**
   a. nadar
   b. pescar
   c. jugar cartas
   d. bailar

3. **to play cards**
   a. jugar al billar
   b. jugar al volibol
   c. jugar al boliche
   d. jugar cartas

4. **to fish**
   a. pescar
   b. nadar
   c. tomar
   d. ir a las fiestas

5. **to read**
   a. comer
   b. tomar
   c. bailar
   d. leer

6. **to bowl**
   a. nadar
   b. bailar
   c. jugar al boliche
   d. jugar al billar

7. **to play billiards**
   a. jugar al billar
   b. jugar al boliche
   c. comer
   d. bailar

8. **to swim**
   a. bailar
   b. comer
   c. nadar
   d. pescar

LA GRAMÁTICA: "YO" Y "I"

Usted ha aprendido a expresar las cosas que le gustan y las que no le gustan usando el verbo *gustar (to like)*. Para expresar que usted efectivamente participa en una actividad, use la palabra "*I*" (yo). Estudie el modelo.

Me gusta escuchar la música.	**I like to listen to music.**
Escucho jazz.	**I listen to jazz.**

Para decir que usted no participa en las actividades, añada "*do not*" antes de la palabra.

Bailo.	**I dance.**
No bailo.	**I do not dance.**

Para preguntarle a alguien en qué actividades él o ella participa, pregunte con "*Do you. . .?*" antes de la palabra.

¿Te gusta mirar la televisión?	**Do you like to watch T.V.?**
¿Miras *Friends?*	**Do you watch *Friends?***
Sí, miro *Friends.*	**Yes, I watch *Friends.***

EJERCICIO DE TRADUCCIÓN

Traduzca al español.

1. I dance. _____

2. I swim. _____

3. I fish. _____

4. I drink. _____

5. I listen to music. _____
_____

6. I play billiards. _____

7. I watch T.V. _____

8. I read. _____

9. I do not dance. _____

10. I do not swim. _____

11. I do not fish. _____

12. I do not drink. _____

13. I do not listen to music. _____
_____

14. I do not play billiards. _____
_____

15. I do not watch T.V. _____
_____

16. I do not read. _____
_____

17. Do you dance? _____

18. Do you swim? _____

19. Do you fish? _____

20. Do you drink? _____

21. Do you listen to music? _____
_____

22. Do you play billiards? _____
_____

23. Do you watch T.V.? _____
_____

24. Do you read? _____
_____

25. Do you dance? _____

EJERCICIO DE ROLE PLAY

A. **¡Hablar siempre de trabajo se pone aburrido!** Averigüe más acerca de las cosas que le interesan a sus compañeros de trabajo preguntando si él o ella participan en estas actividades. Sigue el modelo.

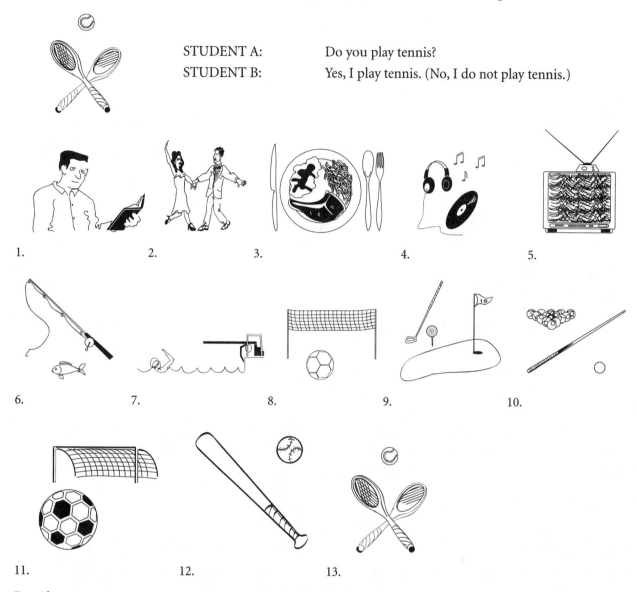

STUDENT A: Do you play tennis?
STUDENT B: Yes, I play tennis. (No, I do not play tennis.)

1.   2.   3.   4.   5.

6.   7.   8.   9.   10.

11.   12.   13.

B. Ahora pregúntense unos a otros con quién (*with whom*) realizan esas actividades. Sigue el modelo.

STUDENT A: With whom do you play tennis?
STUDENT B: I play tennis with my friend.

C. Trabaje con un compañero preguntando y respondiendo cuándo (*when?*) él o ella realiza esas actividades. Sigue el modelo.

STUDENT A: When do you play tennis?
STUDENT B: I play tennis in the summer.

REPASO

Traduzca al español.

1. I like to read. _____

2. I like to be with my family. _____

3. I do not like to go to parties. _____

4. Do you like to play sports? _____

5. Do you like to watch television? _____

6. Do you like to play billiards? _____

7. I listen to music. Do you listen to music? _____

8. I do not watch television. _____

9. I watch golf with my father on Sundays. _____

10. I dance with my wife on Saturdays. _____

11. I play soccer with my supervisors in the fall. _____

12. I fish on the weekends with my friends. _____

13. I play golf in the summer with my boss. _____

14. When do you play volleyball? _____

15. When do you play baseball? _____

Lea el diálogo en voz alta en inglés. Seguidamente tradúzcalo al español.

(Friday, April 22)

Gloria: Hello, Octavio!

Octavio: Hello. How's it going?

Gloria: Fantastic! It's Friday!

Octavio: What do you like to do on Saturdays?

Gloria: I like to be with the family.

Octavio: Ah... Do you like to play soccer?

Gloria: No... I don't like to.

Octavio: Do you like to play volleyball?

Gloria: No... I do not like to play sports.

Octavio: Ah... Do you like to play billiards?

Gloria: Yes... A little. Is there music?

Lea el diálogo en voz alta en español. Seguidamente tradúzcalo al inglés.

(el viernes, el 22 de abril)

Gloria: ¡Hola, Octavio!

Octavio: Hola. ¿Qué tal?

Gloria: ¡Fantástico! ¡Es viernes!

Octavio: ¿Qué te gusta hacer los sábados?

Gloria: Me gusta estar con la familia.

Octavio: Ah... ¿Te gusta jugar al fútbol?

Gloria: No... no me gusta.

Octavio: ¿Te gusta jugar al volibol?

Gloria: No... no me gusta jugar a los deportes.

Octavio: Ah... ¿Te gusta jugar al billar?

Gloria: Sí... un poco. ¿Hay música?

(On Saturday, April 23 at the bar)

Octavio: First. . . Do you want to drink a Margarita?

Gloria: No, thank you. I do not drink.

Octavio: I like to drink. A Margarita, please. . .

Gloria: Is there pizza? I love to eat!

Sergio: Hello! How's it going?

Octavio: Sergio! Hello! How are you?

Sergio: Magnificent!

Octavio: How's the family?

Sergio: Excellent! Thank you.

Octavio: And your brothers?

Sergio: Fine, thank you.

Octavio: I want to introduce you to Gloria.

Sergio: Nice to meet you.

Gloria: Same to you.

Octavio: See you later!

(Octavio and Gloria go to play billiards)

Octavio: Come with me, Gloria. . .

Gloria: I'm nervous.

Octavio: Watch me.

Gloria: (she watches him)

Octavio: Try it.

Gloria: (she hits the ball poorly)

Octavio: It's not correct. . . Do it like me.

Gloria: Help me, Octavio.

Octavio: It's so-so.

Gloria: I don't like to play billiards!

Octavio: Keep trying. . . Fabulous!

Gloria: You are patient, Octavio.

Octavio: Everything else is correct.

Gloria: Thank you very much. Octavio. . . Do you like to dance?

(el sábado, 23 de abril en el bar)

Octavio: Primero. . . ¿Tomas una Margarita?

Gloria: No, gracias. No tomo.

Octavio: Me gusta tomar. Una Margarita, por favor. . .

Gloria: ¿Hay pizza? ¡ Me encanta comer!

Sergio: ¡Hola! ¿Qué tal?

Octavio: ¡Sergio! ¡Hola! ¿Como estás?

Sergio: ¡Magnífico!

Octavio: ¿Cómo está la familia?

Sergio: ¡Excelente! Gracias.

Octavio: ¿Y tus hermanos?

Sergio: Bien, gracias.

Octavio: Quiero presentarte a Gloria.

Sergio: Mucho gusto.

Gloria: Igualmente.

Octavio: ¡Hasta luego!

(Octavio y Gloria van a jugar al billar)

Octavio: Ven conmigo, Gloria. . .

Gloria: Estoy nerviosa jugar al billar.

Octavio: Mírame.

Gloria: (le mira)

Octavio: Trátalo.

Gloria: (golpea mal la bola)

Octavio: No está correcto. . . Házlo como yo.

Gloria: Ayúdame, Octavio.

Octavio: Está así-así.

Gloria: ¡No me gusta jugar al billar!

Octavio: Continua tratando. . . ¡Fabuloso!

Gloria: Eres paciente, Octavio.

Octavio: Todo lo demás está correcto.

Gloria: Muchas gracias. Octavio. . . ¿Te gusta bailar?

LA CULTURA: CULTURAS INDIVIDUALISTAS Y CULTURAS DE GRUPO

En los Estados Unidos la gente habla de "sana competencia." Ya desde que comienzan a estudiar en las escuelas de educación elemental, los estadounidenses compiten en actividades como concursos de deletrear y carreras de relevo. Pasan de las competencias en los juegos infantiles a las competencias por ocupar los mejores empleos. Los Estados Unidos prosperan aprovechando el estímulo de la competencia. Los estadounidenses disfrutan con un ambiente competitivo y piensan que ese ambiente, en su mayor parte, les permite lograr un rendimiento de alta calidad, desarrollar empresas sanas y una economía sólida.

Las expresiones "jugar para ganar" y competir "mano a mano" y "codo con codo" se escuchan comunmente. Los Estados Unidos tienen una sociedad individualista. En los Estados Unidos las recompensas van a las manos de quienes obtienen logros individuales. Entre algunos ejemplos de premios que se otorgan comunmente están los de "Empleado del Mes," "Maestro del Año" y "Jugador Más Valioso." Las empresas sienten la necesidad de contratar asesores comerciales para facilitar seminarios de "Formación de equipos" para sus empleados, de modo que ellos aprendan cómo trabajar mejor como grupo.

El trabajo en grupo es algo natural en muchas otras culturas. En Latinoamérica y gran parte del mundo, los lazos individuales, en comparación con los lazos familiares, son muy flojos. En los países latinos, las personas nacen en colectividades y grupos que pueden formar una especie de familia extendida. La expresión "*hace falta un pueblo para educar a un niño*" se está comprendiendo ahora como un concepto importante en los Estados Unidos. La gente participa mucho más y amplía su identidad formando parte del grupo. Se piensa que la lealtad hacia el grupo debe recompensarse generosamente. La mayoría de los latinos son muy cooperadores y trabajan bien unos con otros en el grupo. Protegen al grupo en su conjunto y con frecuencia le dicen a su supervisor que no quieren a una determinada persona en su grupo porque esa persona hace quedar mal al grupo.

La mayoría de los empleados latinos no son fuertemente competitivos en el sentido de querer superar el rendimiento de sus compañeros de trabajo. No les agrada pasar por encima de sus compañeros para obtener reconocimiento por sus logros individuales superiores. Les gustaría llevarse bien con todos sin haber ganadores o perdedores absolutos. En cambio, en un partido de fútbol, por ejemplo, sí son competitivos, pero en el trabajo, los latinos aprecian un ambiente más cordial y relajado, sin conflictos ni enfrentamientos. Los latinos normalmente evitan las competencias, así como evitan ofrecerse como voluntarios para algo que podría presentarlos negativamente ante los demás. Ellos temen fallar en el intento. En una sociedad latina muy bien entrelazada y orientada hacia el grupo, la reputación que uno tiene con los amigos y los compañeros de trabajo es muy importante.

6

La Salud y La Seguridad

PARTE I   LA SALUD

la cabeza
head

el ojo
eye

el oído
ear

el cuello
neck

el hombro
shoulder

el pecho
chest

el estómago
stomach

la pierna
leg

la rodilla
knee

el tobillo
ankle

los pies
feet

la espalda
back

la sangre
blood

el brazo
arm

el codo
elbow

la mano
hand

los dedos
fingers

EJERCICIO DE CORRESPONDENCIA

Escriba la letra de cada dibujo al lado de la palabra inglesa que corresponde abajo.

a.

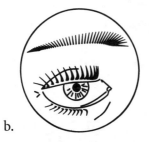
b.

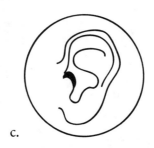
c.

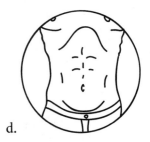
d.

e.

f.

g.

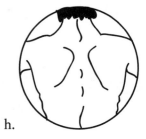
h.

i.

j.

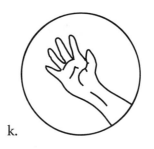
k.

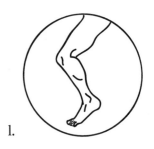
l.

1. _____ blood	7. _____ fingers
2. _____ eye	8. _____ head
3. _____ ankle	9. _____ hand
4. _____ stomach	10. _____ leg
5. _____ ear	11. _____ feet
6. _____ back	12. _____ arm

EJERCICIO DE VOCABULARIO

Escriba la palabra inglesa abajo.

1. _____

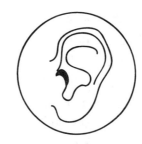

2. _____

3. _____

4. _____

5. _____

6. _____

7. _____

8. _____

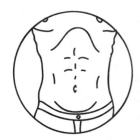

9. _____

10. _____

11. _____

12. _____

EJERCICIO DE CORRESPONDENCIA

Escriba la letra de la palabra en español junto a la palabra inglesa que corresponda a la izquierda.

1. _____ feet	9. _____ stomach	a. la cabeza	i. el codo
2. _____ knee	10. _____ arm	b. el brazo	j. el hombro
3. _____ eye	11. _____ head	c. el estómago	k. el cuello
4. _____ ear	12. _____ chest	d. la pierna	l. el pecho
5. _____ hand	13. _____ fingers	e. el tobillo	m. el oído
6. _____ elbow	14. _____ back	f. los pies	n. el ojo
7. _____ ankle	15. _____ shoulder	g. la rodilla	o. los dedos
8. _____ leg	16. _____ neck	h. la mano	p. la espalda

CRUCIGRAMAS

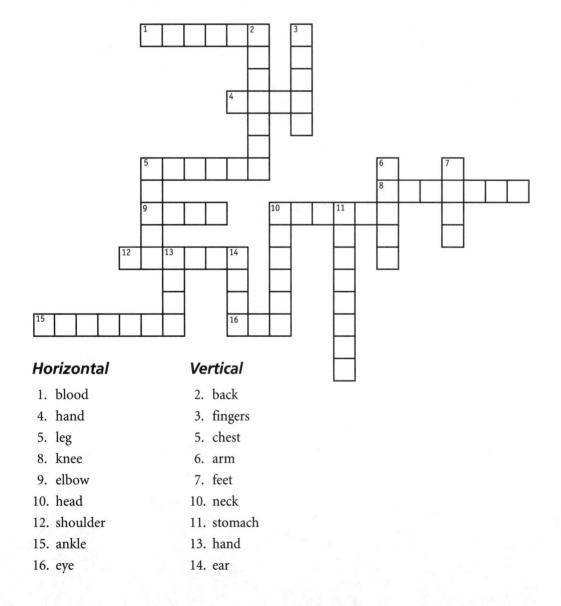

Horizontal

1. blood
4. hand
5. leg
8. knee
9. elbow
10. head
12. shoulder
15. ankle
16. eye

Vertical

2. back
3. fingers
5. chest
6. arm
7. feet
10. neck
11. stomach
13. hand
14. ear

Horizontal

1. cuello
3. espalda
5. hombro
7. rodilla
9. ojo
10. pies
11. brazo
12. pierna
13. sangre
15. mano
16. oído

Vertical

2. pecho
4. tobillo
5. estómago
6. cabeza
8. codo
14. dedo

EJERCICIO DE TRADUCCIÓN

Traduzca al inglés.

1. los pies _____
2. la mano _____
3. la rodilla _____
4. los dedos _____
5. la cabeza _____
6. la sangre _____
7. el oído _____
8. el hombro _____
9. la espalda _____
10. el pecho _____
11. el brazo _____
12. el codo _____
13. la pierna _____
14. el tobillo _____
15. el ojo _____

Traduzca al español.

1. feet _____
2. hand _____
3. fingers _____
4. blood _____
5. head _____
6. eye _____
7. arm _____
8. ear _____
9. shoulder _____
10. chest _____
11. back _____
12. ankle _____
13. knee _____
14. stomach _____
15. leg _____

OPCIONES MÚLTIPLES

Marque con un círculo la letra de la respuesta correcta.

1. **fingers**
   a. los dedos
   b. los pies
   c. los brazos
   d. la pierna

2. **ankle**
   a. la rodilla
   b. la pierna
   c. el tobillo
   d. el brazo

3. **eye**
   a. la sangre
   b. la mano
   c. el oído
   d. el ojo

4. **head**
   a. la cabeza
   b. la espalda

   c. la pierna
   d. el hombro

5. **ear**
   a. el ojo
   b. el oído
   c. la rodilla
   d. el pecho

6. **back**
   a. la cabeza
   b. el pecho
   c. el estómago
   d. la espalda

7. **blood**
   a. el pulgar
   b. el cuello
   c. el codo
   d. la sangre

8. **feet**
   a. los pies
   b. los dedos
   c. la cabeza
   d. la pierna

9. **hand**
   a. la mano
   b. el codo
   c. el pecho
   d. el tobillo

10. **knee**
    a. el brazo
    b. el tobillo
    c. la rodilla
    d. el cuello

LA GRAMÁTICA

El verbo *doler* significa "*to hurt,*" "*to ache.*"

EJERCICIO DE ROLE PLAY

Imagínese que su compañero de trabajo se ha lastimado en el trabajo. Pregúntele qué le duele. Sigue el modelo.

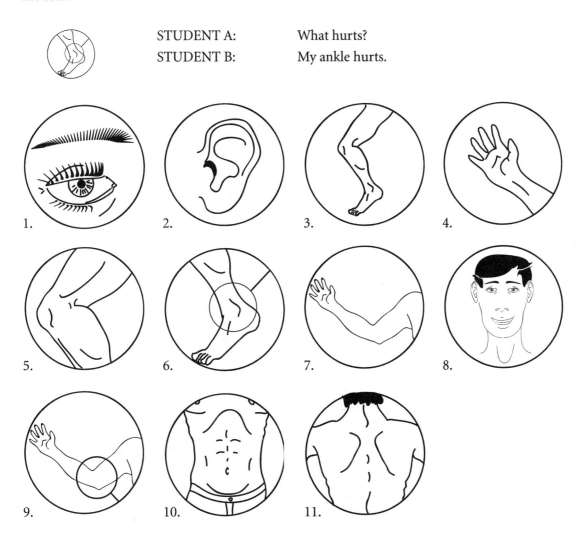

| | STUDENT A: | What hurts? |
| | STUDENT B: | My ankle hurts. |

1.
2.
3.
4.
5.
6.
7.
8.
9.
10.
11.

EJERCICIO DE TRADUCCIÓN

Traduzca al español.

1. What hurts? _____

2. My head hurts. _____

3. My eye hurts. _____

4. What hurts? _____

5. My ankle hurts. _____

6. My knee hurts. _____

7. What hurts? _____

8. My stomach hurts. _____

9. My back hurts. _____

10. What hurts? _____

PARTE II   LA SEGURIDAD

el extinguidor
fire extinguisher

el botiquín
first aid kit

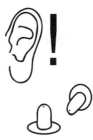

los tapones para los oídos
earplugs

la gorra
baseball cap

el casco de seguridad
safety helmet

los lentes de seguridad
safety glasses

el uniforme
uniform

las botas
boots

los guantes
gloves

usa	**use**	¡Quema!	**Burns!**
lleva	**wear**	Presta atención.	**Pay attention.**
lava	**wash**	Ten cuidado.	**Be careful.**
¡Peligro!	**Danger!**	Maneja despacio.	**Drive slowly.**
¡Aviso!	**Warning!**	Busca refugio.	**Seek shelter.**
¡Atención!	**Attention!**	No toques las navajas.	**Don't touch the blades.**
¡Caliente!	**Hot!**		

EJERCICIO DE CORRESPONDENCIA

Escriba la letra de cada dibujo al lado de la palabra inglesa que corresponde abajo.

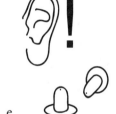 a.

 b.

 c.

 d.

 e.

 f.

 g.

 h.

 i.

1. _____ fire extinguisher

2. _____ safety helmet

3. _____ gloves

4. _____ uniform

5. _____ boots

6. _____ first aid kit

7. _____ safety goggles

8. _____ baseball cap

9. _____ earplugs

EJERCICIO DE VOCABULARIO

Escriba la palabra inglesa abajo.

1. _____

2. _____

3. _____

4. _____

5. _____

6. _____

7. _____

8. _____

9. _____

EJERCICIO DE CORRESPONDENCIA

Escriba la letra de la palabra en español junto a la palabra inglesa que corresponda a la izquierda.

1. _____ uniform   a. el extinguidor
2. _____ baseball cap   b. los tapones para los oídos
3. _____ gloves   c. el uniforme
4. _____ safety glasses   d. el botiquín
5. _____ safety helmet   e. los lentes de seguridad
6. _____ boots   f. los guantes
7. _____ earplugs   g. el casco de seguridad
8. _____ fire extinguisher   h. las botas
9. _____ first aid kit   i. la gorra

CRUCIGRAMAS

Horizontal

2. boots
4. gloves
7. first aid
9. safety helmet

Vertical

1. uniform
3. ear plugs
5. fire extinguisher
6. safety glasses
8. baseball cap

Horizontal

4. tapones para los oídos
7. botas
9. casco de seguridad

Vertical

1. gorra
2. uniforme
3. extinguidor
5. guantes
6. botiquín
8. lentes de seguridad

EJERCICIO DE TRADUCCIÓN

Traduzca al inglés.

1. el botiquín _____
2. los guantes _____
3. el casco de seguridad _____
4. el uniforme _____
5. la gorra _____
6. los lentes de seguridad _____
7. los tapones para los oídos _____
8. las botas _____
9. el extinguidor _____

Traduzca al español.

1. first aid kit _____
2. fire extinguisher _____
3. baseball cap _____
4. boots _____
5. gloves _____
6. earplugs _____
7. safety glasses _____
8. safety helmet _____
9. uniform _____

OPCIONES MÚLTIPLES

Marque con un círculo la letra de la respuesta correcta.

1. **safety helmet**
   a. los guantes
   b. los tapones para los oídos
   c. el casco de seguridad
   d. los lentes de seguridad

2. **boots**
   a. las botas
   b. las guantes
   c. la gorra
   d. el uniforme

3. **fire extinguisher**
   a. los lentes de seguridad
   b. el extinguidor
   c. los lentes de seguridad
   d. el botiquín

4. **gloves**
   a. las botas
   b. el uniforme
   c. la gorra
   d. las guantes

5. **safety glasses**
   a. los guantes
   b. las botas
   c. el casco de seguridad
   d. los lentes de seguridad

6. **baseball cap**
   a. las botas
   b. la gorra
   c. el uniforme
   d. las guantes

7. **first aid kit**
   a. el botiquín
   b. los lentes de seguridad
   c. el extinguidor
   d. el casco de seguridad

8. **earplugs**
   a. el casco de seguridad
   b. los lentes de seguridad
   c. los tapones para los oídos
   d. las guantes

EJERCICIO DE CORRESPONDENCIA

Escriba la letra de la palabra en español junto a la palabra inglesa que corresponda a la izquierda.

1. _____ Be careful.
2. _____ Danger!
3. _____ Pay attention.
4. _____ Warning!
5. _____ Drive slowly.
6. _____ Hot!
7. _____ Seek shelter.
8. _____ Burns!
9. _____ Don't touch the blades.

a. ¡Aviso!
b. ¡Quema!
c. Busca refugio.
d. ¡Caliente!
e. No toques las navajas.
f. Ten cuidado.
g. Presta atención.
h. ¡Peligro!
i. Maneja despacio.

CRUCIGRAMAS

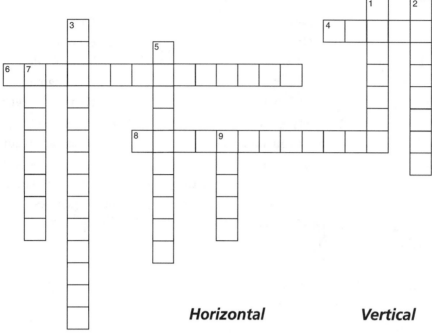

Horizontal

4. Burns!
6. Drive slowly!
8. Seek shelter!

Vertical

1. Danger!
2. Hot!
3. Pay attention!
5. Be careful!
7. Attention!
9. Warning!

Horizontal

5. ¡Peligro!
6. ¡Caliente!
7. ¡Ten cuidado!
8. ¡Aviso!

Vertical

1. ¡Busque refugio!
2. ¡Quema!
3. ¡Atención!
4. Presta atención.
5. ¡Maneja despacio!

EJERCICIO DE TRADUCCIÓN

Traduzca al español.

1. Drive slowly. _____

2. Pay attention. _____

3. Burns! _____

4. Hot! _____

5. Be careful. _____

6. Don't touch the blades. _____

7. Warning! _____

8. Danger! _____

9. Seek shelter. _____

Traduzca al inglés.

1. ¡Quema! _____

2. Busca refugio. _____

3. ¡Peligro! _____

4. Ten cuidado. _____

5. ¡Caliente! _____

6. No toques las navajas. _____

7. ¡Aviso! _____

8. Maneja despacio. _____

9. Presta atención. _____

OPCIONES MÚLTIPLES

Marque con un círculo la letra de la respuesta correcta.

1. **Danger!**
   a. ¡Quema!
   b. ¡Peligro!
   c. ¡Aviso!
   d. ¡Caliente!

2. **Warning!**
   a. ¡Quema!
   b. ¡Peligro!
   c. ¡Aviso!
   d. ¡Caliente!

3. **Hot!**
   a. ¡Quema!
   b. ¡Peligro!
   c. ¡Aviso!
   d. ¡Caliente!

4. **Burns!**
   a. ¡Quema!
   b. ¡Peligro!
   c. ¡Aviso!
   d. ¡Caliente!

5. **Be careful.**
   a. Busque refugio.
   b. Ten cuidado.
   c. Presta atención.
   d. Maneja despacio.

6. **Pay attention.**
   a. Busque refugio.
   b. No toques las navajas.
   c. Presta atención.
   d. Maneja despacio.

7. **Drive slowly.**
   a. Maneja despacio.
   b. Busque refugio.
   c. Ten cuidado.
   d. No toques las navajas.

8. **Don't touch the blades.**
   a. Presta atención.
   b. Busque refugio.
   c. Ten cuidado.
   d. No toques las navajas.

EJERCICIO DE TRADUCCIÓN

Traduzca al español.

1. What hurts? _____

2. My ankle hurts. _____

3. My back hurts. _____

4. Does your stomach hurt? _____

5. Wear the safety helmet and ear plugs. _____

6. Wear the uniform and baseball cap. _____

7. Wash the uniform. _____

8. Wear the gloves and boots. _____

9. Be careful. _____

10. Drive slowly! _____

11. Seek shelter! _____

12. Pay attention! _____

13. Don't touch the blades! _____

14. Danger! _____

15. Hot! _____

REPASO

Lea el diálogo en voz alta en inglés. Seguidamente tradúzcalo al español.

Jill: Don't you like to be with the family?

Mark: Yes . . . but* it's Saturday . . . I play baseball at 3:00.

Jill: And Sunday? You play golf?

Mark: Yes. I play at 8:00.

Jill: You are not very cooperative. It's important, Mark.

Mark: Are you in a bad mood, Jill?

Jill: Yes . . . I am angry and sad!

Mark: Where is my uniform, hat and glove?

Jill: You are not very organized, Mark.

Mark: What time is it?

Jill: It's 2:30.

Mark: See you later.

Jill: Drive slowly!

Lea el diálogo en voz alta en español. Seguidamente tradúzcalo al inglés.

Jill: ¿No te gusta estar con la familia?

Mark: Sí, pero* es sábado . . . juego al béisbol a las tres.

Jill: ¿Y el domingo? ¿Juegas golf?

Mark: Sí. Juego a las ocho.

Jill: No eres muy cooperativo. Es importante, Mark.

Mark: ¿Estás de mal humor, Jill?

Jill: Sí . . . ¡Estoy enojada y triste!

Mark: ¿Dónde está mi uniforme, gorra y guante?

Jill: No eres muy organizado, Mark.

Mark: ¿Qué hora es?

Jill: Son las dos y media.

Mark: Hasta luego.

Jill: ¡Maneja despacio!

(at the baseball field)

Jim: Pay attention!

Mark: Be careful!

(two players collide)

Jim: Ay! . . . I'm not well. I feel bad.

Mark: What hurts?

Jim: My arm hurts.

Mark: Does your elbow or hand hurt?

Jim: My hand.

Mark: Your fingers or your thumb?

Jim: My thumb. Mark . . . What hurts?

Mark: My leg.

Jim: Does your ankle or your knee hurt?

Mark: My knee.

Jim: The knee is bad.

Mark: I'm furious. I can't** play golf on Sunday.

Jim: You can*** be with your family . . . you can watch television and play cards.

Mark: Yes . . . yes . . . Where is the first aid kit?

  *but – pero
 **I can't – No puedo
***you can – Puedes

(en el campo de béisbol)

Jim: ¡Presta atención!

Mark: Ten cuidado!

(dos jugadores chocan)

Jim: ¡Ay! . . . no estoy bien. Estoy mal.

Mark: ¿Qué te duele?

Jim: Me duele el brazo.

Mark: ¿Te duele el codo o la mano?

Jim: La mano.

Mark: ¿Los dedos o el pulgar?

Jim: El pulgar. Mark . . . ¿Qué te duele?

Mark: La pierna.

Jim: ¿Te duele el tobillo o la rodilla?

Mark: La rodilla.

Jim: La rodilla está mal.

Mark: Estoy furioso. No puedo** jugar al golf el domingo.

Jim: Puedes*** estar con la familia . . . puedes mirar la televisión y jugar cartas.

Mark: Sí . . . sí . . . ¿Dónde está el botiquín?

  *pero – [but]
 **No puedo – I can't
***Puedes – you can

Traduzca al español.

1. What's your name? _____

2. Where are you from? _____

3. Come with me. _____

4. Do it like me. _____

5. You're a hard worker! _____

6. Magnificent! _____

7. Where is . . . _____

8. How many? _____

9. When? _____

10. Monday, Tuesday, Wednesday _____

11. The women are furious! _____

12. The foreman is worried and nervous. _____

13. I'm in a good mood! _____

14. Do you like to play billiards and bowl? _____

15. Do you like to play cards and go to parties? _____

16. I like to listen to music and I like to dance. _____

LA CULTURA: ESTILOS DE COMUNICACIÓN

En la cultura latina, al igual que en muchas otras culturas, guardar las apariencias es fundamental. Todas las respuestas se dan para evitar herir los sentimientos de los demás. Como consecuencia de esta actitud, las respuestas evasivas o a medias y las "mentiritas blancas" son actos comunes. Estas respuestas pueden producir grandes confusiones y problemas para un supervisor estadounidense que haya sido educado para ser abierto, franco, directo y sobre todo, honesto, en las situaciones propias del lugar de trabajo.

En las culturas latinas, "sí" puede significar "sí," "quizá" e incluso "no." Los latinos no siempre dicen lo que piensan ni piensan precisamente lo que dicen. Los latinos tienden a dar a entender las cosas, sugerir o recomendar en lugar de plantarse de frente y decir lo que piensan; los latinos entienden que uno nunca puede decir las cosas como son y ser cortante, puesto que al hacerlo se puede molestar a los demás.

Mantener la armonía y guardar las apariencias son factores fundamentales en la sociedad latina. Se debe alterar la verdad, si la verdad trastorna la armonía o puede hacer que una persona quede mal. Con frecuencia un latino le dice a su supervisor lo que el latino cree que su supervisor desea escuchar. No siempre es apropiado no estar de acuerdo o cuestionar las cosas (eso trastorna la armonía) o decir "no" a los compañeros de trabajo. Proteger y reforzar las relaciones y los lazos personales es la meta del proceso de comunicación entre los latinos.

En los Estados Unidos, "sí" quiere decir "sí" y "no" significa "no." Los supervisores dicen lo que piensan y piensan lo que dicen. Uno no tiene que interpretar lo que se ha dicho. En los Estados Unidos, es importante "decir las cosas como son." Es menos probable que los supervisores den a entender algo; ellos tienden más bien a expresar específicamente lo que opinan. Una mujer latina muy conocida e interesada en el campo de las comunicaciones considera que la gente en los Estados Unidos es sincera.

En los Estados Unidos decir la verdad se aprecia más que proteger los sentimientos de una persona. ¡La expresión "*la honestidad es la mejor política*" es tan común en la sociedad estadounidense que fue la pregunta más fácil por $100 en el concurso de televisión "*¿Quién quiere ser millonario?*"! Dar y recibir información eficazmente es la principal meta del proceso de comunicación. En los Estados Unidos está bien no estar de acuerdo y cuestionar los puntos de vista de su jefe o sus compañeros de trabajo.

Si un latino cometa un error, vale la pena que él comprenda que no quedará mal con su supervisor si dice la verdad. Lo más probable es que ese latino pierda el respeto de su supervisor si no admite su error y ese error se descubre más adelante de todos modos.

Para llegar a la verdad con los latinos, es importante tener una buena relación de confianza con ellos. Un supervisor estadounidense debe tener presente que un latino no va a sincerarse ante la gente con la cual no tenga una relación estrecha. Una vez que exista ese lazo entre ellos, los supervisores se dan cuenta que sus compañeros de trabajo y sus subordinados latinos se vuelven más abiertos y francos en sus respuestas.

7

Las Herramientas y Los Equipos

PARTE I   LAS HERRAMIENTAS Y LOS EQUIPOS

la sopladora
blower

la escoba
broom

el cepillo
push broom

el serrucho de gas
gas chainsaw

la podadera
pruner

la manguera
hose

el rastrillo de hojas
leaf rake

el rastrillo de tierra
soil rake

la horca
pitchfork

el rototiller
rototiller

la pala
shovel

el marro, el mazo
sledgehammer

el pico
pick

la máquina
lawnmower

la carretilla
wheelbarrow

las llantas
tires

el aceite
oil

la gasolina
gas

EJERCICIO DE CORRESPONDENCIA

Escriba la letra de cada dibujo al lado de la palabra inglesa que corresponda abajo.

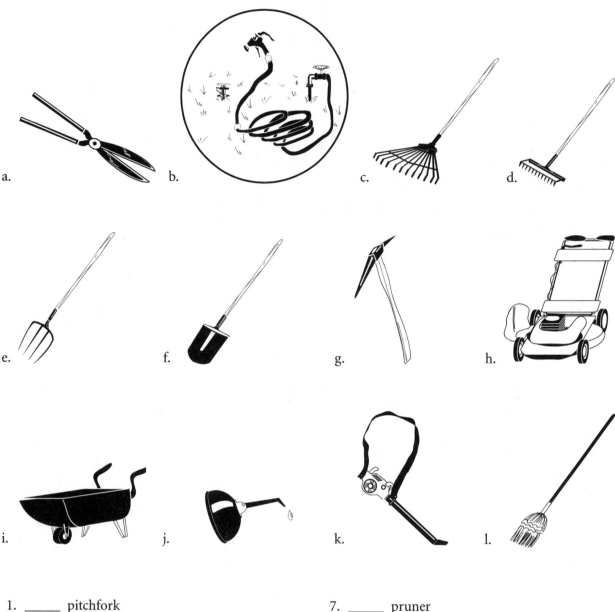

a.

b.

c.

d.

e.

f.

g.

h.

i.

j.

k.

l.

1. _____ pitchfork

2. _____ oil

3. _____ leaf rake

4. _____ wheelbarrow

5. _____ hose

6. _____ lawnmower

7. _____ pruner

8. _____ pick

9. _____ broom

10. _____ shovel

11. _____ blower

12. _____ soil rake

EJERCICIO DE VOCABULARIO

Escriba la palabra inglesa abajo.

1. _____

2. _____

3. _____

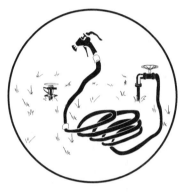

4. _____

5. _____

6. _____

7. _____

8. _____

9. _____

10. _____

11. _____

12. _____

EJERCICIO DE CORRESPONDENCIA

Escriba la letra de la palabra en español junto a la palabra inglesa que corresponda a la izquierda.

1. _____ blower
2. _____ broom
3. _____ gas chainsaw
4. _____ hand pruner
5. _____ hose
6. _____ rake
7. _____ pitchfork
8. _____ rototiller
9. _____ shovel
10. _____ sledgehammer
11. _____ pick
12. _____ lawnmower
13. _____ wheelbarrow
14. _____ tires
15. _____ oil
16. _____ gas

a. la horca
b. el aceite
c. la gasolina
d. las llantas
e. el rototiller
f. la carretilla
g. la sopladora
h. la manguera
i. el marro, el mazo
j. la pala
k. el rastrillo
l. la podadera
m. el pico
n. la máquina
o. la escoba
p. el serrucho de gas

CRUCIGRAMAS

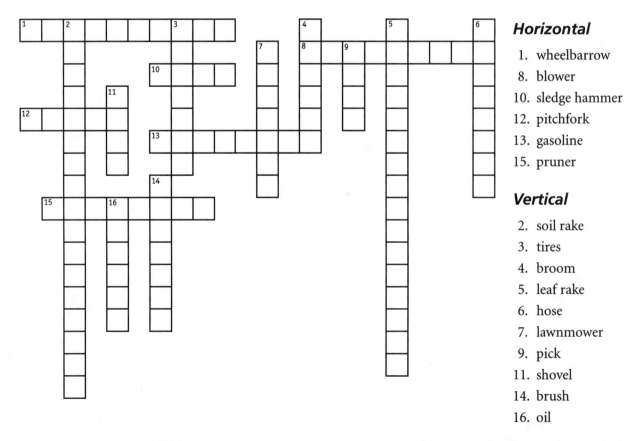

Horizontal

1. wheelbarrow
8. blower
10. sledge hammer
12. pitchfork
13. gasoline
15. pruner

Vertical

2. soil rake
3. tires
4. broom
5. leaf rake
6. hose
7. lawnmower
9. pick
11. shovel
14. brush
16. oil

Horizontal

1. carretilla
4. llantas
5. rastrillo de tierra
7. horca
8. mazo
9. podadera
10. gasolina
12. escoba
14. pala
15. máquina

Vertical

2. sopladora
3. pico
6. rastrillo de hojas
9. cepillo
11. manguera
13. aceite

EJERCICIO DE TRADUCCIÓN

Traduzca al inglés.

1. la sopladora _____
2. el aceite _____
3. la gasolina _____
4. la manguera _____
5. el rototiller _____
6. la carretilla _____
7. la horca _____
8. las llantas _____
9. el marro, el mazo _____
10. el serrucho de gas _____
11. el rastrillo _____
12. el pico _____
13. la podadera _____
14. la escoba _____
15. el cepillo _____
16. la pala _____

Traduzca al español.

1. pruner _____
2. hose _____
3. rake _____
4. pitchfork _____
5. rototiller _____
6. blower _____
7. broom _____
8. push broom _____
9. gas chainsaw _____
10. lawnmower _____
11. wheelbarrow _____
12. shovel _____
13. sledgehammer _____
14. pick _____
15. tires _____
16. oil _____
17. gas _____

OPCIONES MÚLTIPLES

Marque con un círculo la letra de la respuesta correcta.

1. **pruner**
   a. el rastrillo
   b. el pico
   c. la podadera
   d. el aceite

2. **hose**
   a. la sopladora
   b. el aceite
   c. la gasolina
   d. la manguera

3. **wheelbarrow**
   a. la carretilla
   b. la horca
   c. las llantas
   d. el marro, el mazo

4. **blower**
   a. la sopladora
   b. la podadera
   c. la serrucho de gas
   d. el marro, el mazo

5. **broom**
   a. el rastrillo
   b. el pico
   c. la podadera
   d. la escoba

6 **rake**
   a. el rastrillo
   b. el pico
   c. la podadera
   d. la sopladora

7. **oil**
   a. la sopladora
   b. el aceite
   c. la gasolina
   d. la manguera

8. **pitchfork**
   a. la horca
   b. el pico
   c. la pala
   d. la escoba

LA GRAMÁTICA

Dame . . .   **Give me . . .**
Dámelo/Dámela: **Give it to me.**

EJERCICIO ORAL

Muchas organizaciones numeran sus equipos. Pídale a su compañero que le pase una herramienta. Sigue el modelo.

STUDENT A:	Give me the pick.
STUDENT B:	Five?
STUDENT A:	Yes. Give it to me. Thank you.

1.

2.

3.

4.

5.

6.

7.

8.

9.

10.

PARTE II   TÉRMINOS DE ACCIÓN

Grupo 1		**Grupo 2**	
lava	**wash**	dame	**give me**
guarda	**put away**	dale	**give him**
usa	**use**	pon	**put**
carga	**load**	limpia	**clean**
descarga	**unload**	trae	**bring**
mezcla	**mix**	consigue	**get**
		No sirve.	**It doesn't work.**
		Está roto.	**It's broken.**

GRUPO 1

Ejercicio de Correspondencia

Escriba la letra de la palabra en español junto a la palabra inglesa que corresponda a la izquierda.

1. _____ wash	a. descarga
2. _____ use	b. mezcla
3. _____ load	c. lava
4. _____ put away	d. guarda
5. _____ unload	e. carga
6. _____ mix	f. usa

Traduzca al inglés.

1. carga _____

2. mezcla _____

3. usa _____

4. descarga _____

5. lava _____

6. guarda _____

Traduzca al español.

1. put away _____

2. wash _____

3. unload _____

4. mix _____

5. load _____

6. use _____

GRUPO 2

Ejercicio de Correspondencia

Escriba la letra de la palabra en español junto a la palabra inglesa que corresponda a la izquierda.

1. _____ get		a.	trae
2. _____ give me		b.	pon
3. _____ clean		c.	dale
4. _____ put		d.	consigue
5. _____ give him		e.	limpia
6. _____ bring		f.	dame

Traduzca al inglés.

1. consigue _____

2. limpia _____

3. dame _____

4. dale _____

5. trae _____

6. pon _____

Traduzca al español.

1. bring _____

2. get _____

3. give me _____

4. give him _____

5. put _____

6. clean _____

EJERCICIO DE CORRESPONDENCIA

Escriba la letra de la palabra en español junto a la palabra inglesa que corresponda a la izquierda.

1. _____ wash		a.	carga
2. _____ bring		b.	regresa
3. _____ load		c.	descarga
4. _____ use		d.	usa
5. _____ unload		e.	trae
6. _____ return		f.	limpia
7. _____ put away		g.	lava
8. _____ give me		h.	consigue
9. _____ get		i.	dame
10. _____ clean		j.	guarda
11. _____ give him		k.	mezcla
12. _____ mix		l.	dale

CRUCIGRAMAS

Horizontal

2. unload
6. bring
7. clean
8. load

Vertical

1. use
3. get
4. put away
5. give me

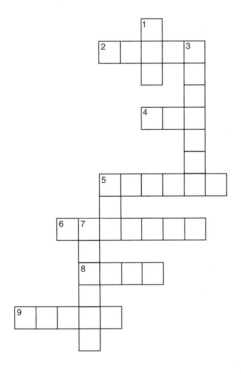

Horizontal

2. trae
4. usa
5. dame
6. guarda
8. carga
9. limpia

Vertical

1. mezcla
3. dale
5. consigue
7. descarga

OPCIONES MÚLTIPLES

Marque con un círculo la letra de la respuesta correcta.

1. get
- a. lava
- b. guarda
- c. consigue
- d. dame

2. load
- a. carga
- b. descarga
- c. dame
- d. dale

3. use
- a. trae
- b. mezcla
- c. pon
- d. usa

4. put away
- a. lava
- b. guarda
- c. consigue
- d. dame

5. give him
- a. carga
- b. descarga
- c. dame
- d. dale

6. wash
- a. lava
- b. guarda
- c. consigue
- d. dame

7. bring
- a. trae
- b. mezcla
- c. pon
- d. usa

8. unload
- a. carga
- b. descarga
- c. dame
- d. dale

9. put
- a. trae
- b. mezcla
- c. pon
- d. usa

10. give me
- a. dame
- b. dale
- c. usa
- d. pon

EJERCICIO DE TRADUCCIÓN

Traduzca al inglés.

1. lava _____
2. usa _____
3. regresa _____
4. guarda _____
5. carga _____
6. limpia _____
7. descarga _____
8. trae _____
9. consigue _____
10. dame _____
11. dale _____
12. mezcla _____

Traduzca al español.

1. load _____
2. unload _____
3. bring _____
4. wash _____
5. use _____
6. put away _____
7. clean _____
8. give me _____
9. get _____
10. return _____
11. give him _____
12. mix _____

REPASO

Traduzca al inglés.

1. Lava la carretilla. _____
2. Usa la sopladora. _____
3. Devuelve el mazo. _____
4. Guarda el rastrillo. _____
5. Carga la manguera. _____
6. Lava las palas. _____
7. Descarga la máquina. _____
8. Trae el serrucho de gas. _____
9. Consigue el pico. _____
10. Dame la pala. _____
11. Mezcla el aceite y la gasolina. _____
12. Dale el cepillo. _____

Traduzca al español.

1. Load the lawnmower. _____
2. Unload the wheelbarrow. _____
3. Bring the hose. _____
4. Wash the shovel. _____
5. Use the pick. _____
6. Put away the rake. _____
7. Mix the oil and gas. _____
8. Give me the gas chainsaw. _____
9. Get the pruner. _____
10. Use the broom. _____
11. Use the push broom. _____
12. Give him the blower. _____

Lea el diálogo en voz alta en inglés. Seguidamente tradúzcalo al español.

Frank: Come with me.

Domingo: (follows Frank to the garage)

Frank: Help me.

Domingo: Yes. You're the boss!

Frank: Load the blowers.

Domingo: And the rakes?

Frank: Yes. Load the shovels and the brushes.

Domingo: And the lawnmowers?

Frank: Yes . . . mix the oil and the gas.

Domingo: Okay.

Frank: Oh . . . and the pruners. Thank you.
(later at the site)

Domingo: Unload the lawnmowers?

Frank: Yes . . . Watch me. (starts the lawn mower . . .)

Domingo: Good work.

Lea el diálogo en voz alta en español. Seguidamente tradúzcalo al inglés.

Frank: Ven conmigo.

Domingo: (Sigue a Frank al garaje)

Frank: Ayúdame.

Domingo: Sí. ¡Eres el jefe!

Frank: Carga las sopladoras.

Domingo: ¿Y los rastrillos?

Frank: Sí. Carga las palas y los cepillos.

Domingo: ¿Y las máquinas?

Frank: Sí . . . mezcla el aceite y la gasolina.

Domingo: Okay.

Frank: Ay . . . y las podaderas. Gracias.
(más tarde en el sitio)

Domingo: ¿Descargo las máquinas?

Frank: Sí . . . Mírame. (arranca la máquina . . .)

Domingo: Buen trabajo.

Frank: Thank you. Do it like me.

Domingo: I'm nervous . . . Ay!

Frank: Are you okay? Does your foot hurt?

Domingo: No . . . no . . . I feel bad.

Frank: Please . . . Don't touch the blades!

Domingo: Okay. (Looks at his foot . . . gets on the mower.)

Frank: Domingo . . . Try it.

Domingo: Is this okay?

Frank: Keep trying, Domingo.

Domingo: Is this correct?

Frank: Yes. Excellent!

Domingo: (Drives off recklessly.)

Frank: Drive slowly!

Domingo: HELP ME!

Frank: Gracias. Házlo como yo.

Domingo: Estoy nervioso . . . ¡Ay!

Frank: ¿Estás bien? Te duele el pie?

Domingo: No . . . no . . . estoy mal.

Frank: Por favor . . . ¡No toques las navajas!

Domingo: Okay. (Mira el pie . . . sube la máquina.)

Frank: Domingo . . . Trátalo.

Domingo: ¿Está bien?

Frank: Continua tratando, Domingo.

Domingo: ¿Está correcto?

Frank: Sí. Excelente!

Domingo: (Maneja muy mal.)

Frank: ¡Maneja despacio!

Domingo: ¡AYÚDAME!

Traduzca al español.

1. Hello. Welcome. _____

2. I'd like to introduce you to . . . _____

3. Nice to meet you. Same to you. _____

4. Watch me. Do it like me. _____

5. Try it. Continue trying. _____

6. You're a hard worker! _____

7. Thursday Friday Saturday _____

8. February March November _____

9. There is a party. How many pizzas? _____

10. I play golf. Do you like to play golf? _____

11. The crew is hardworking! _____

12. My brother is the foreman. _____

13. Does your ankle hurt? _____

14. There is blood. _____

15. Where is the first aid kit? _____

LA CULTURA: EL ENTRENAMIENTO

El entrenamiento eficaz es uno de los aspectos cruciales en cualquier organización. En los países latinoamericanos, este entrenamiento es extremadamente teórico y hay pocos programas estructurados. Sin embargo, en los Estados Unidos el entrenamiento es concreto, específico y muy práctico. Los programas estructurados de entrenamiento se emplean ampliamente en las compañías de éxito.

Al dar entrenamiento, un aspecto que debe considerarse es la actitud de un empleado hacia la incertidumbre. Esto varía en cada cultura. En los Estados Unidos, la gente no tiene miedo de arriesgarse o fracasar. Cuando se les pide que se ofrezcan como voluntarios frente a un grupo, muchos estadounidenses optan por dar un paso al frente para participar. Los estadounidenses aprenden con el método de ensayo y error, y así mejoran sus habilidades, productos y servicios.

En muchas culturas latinas, asumir riesgos y fracasar frente a los demás son cosas que deben evitarse de ser posible. Pida la participación de un voluntario entre un grupo de latinos y verá que la inmensa mayoría de ellos agachará la cabeza. Un latino no intenta hacer algo nuevo a menos que sepa que puede hacerlo. La mujer o el hombre latino puede tener un sentimiento de inseguridad acerca de sus habilidades. Si fracasa, es posible que no lo intente nuevamente. En su mayoría, los latinos son receptivos y están ansiosos por aprender nuevos métodos y agradecen mucho la oportunidad de recibir entrenamiento. Sin embargo, es posible que se sientan desanimados si piensan que la única forma en que se les enseña a hacer una tarea es la "manera americana."

Al dar entrenamiento y desarrollar las aptitudes de un empleado inseguro de sí mismo en cualquier cultura es importante aumentar su autoestima. Alabe al empleado por cada paso que dé en sentido positivo, por más pequeño que sea el avance, de tal forma que adquiera confianza en sus habilidades. Ellos realizarán esa tarea mucho mejor si no se sienten nerviosos por la posibilidad de cometer un error.

8

El Mantenimiento de Terrenos

PARTE I EL MANTENIMIENTO DE TERRENOS

los arbustos
shrubs, bushes

las ramas
branches

el cortado
clippings

las flores
flowers

el zacate, el pasto
grass

el hoyo
hole

las hojas
leaves

las plantas
plants

las raíces
roots

las semillas
seeds

la tierra
soil

los árboles
trees

las hierbas
weeds

EJERCICIO DE CORRESPONDENCIA

Escriba la letra de cada dibujo al lado de la palabra inglesa que corresponda abajo.

a.   b.   c.   d.

e.   f.   g.   h.

i.   j.   k.   l.

1. _____ hole	7. _____ branches
2. _____ plants	8. _____ soil
3. _____ grass	9. _____ leaves
4. _____ roots	10. _____ seeds
5. _____ weeds	11. _____ trees
6. _____ flowers	12. _____ shrubs

EJERCICIO DE VOCABULARIO

Escriba la palabra inglesa abajo.

1. _____

2. _____

3. _____

4. _____

5. _____

6. _____

7. _____

8. _____

9. _____

10. _____

11. _____

12. _____

EJERCICIO DE CORRESPONDENCIA

Escriba la letra de la palabra en español junto a la palabra inglesa que corresponda a la izquierda.

1. _____ flowers		a. tierra
2. _____ weeds		b. hierbas
3. _____ soil		c. arbustos
4. _____ shrubs, bushes		d. plantas
5. _____ grass		e. semillas
6. _____ plants		f. raíces
7. _____ leaves		g. flores
8. _____ seeds		h. ramas
9. _____ branches		i. hojas
10. _____ clippings		j. zacate, pasto
11. _____ roots		k. árboles
12. _____ trees		l. cortado

CRUCIGRAMAS

Horizontal

1. shrubs
3. roots
5. branches
10. trees
11. plant
12. leaves

Vertical

2. soil
4. grass
6. seeds
7. weeds
8. flowers
9. hole

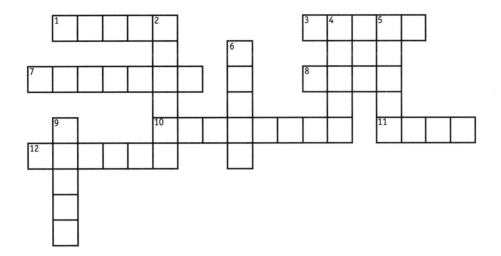

Horizontal

1. árboles
3. zacate
7. flores
8. hoyo
10. ramas
11. tierra
12. hojas

Vertical

2. arbustos
4. raíces
5. semillas
6. planta
9. hierbas

EJERCICIO DE TRADUCCIÓN

Traduzca al inglés.

1. los árboles _____
2. las hojas _____
3. el pasto, el zacate _____
4. las ramas _____
5. los arbustos _____
6. las raíces _____
7. el cortado _____
8. las flores _____
9. el hoyo _____
10. las plantas _____
11. la tierra _____
12. las hierbas _____

Traduzca al español.

1. trees _____
2. leaves _____
3. shrubs, bushes _____
4. flowers _____
5. seeds _____
6. branches _____
7. weeds _____
8. grass _____
9. clippings _____
10. plants _____
11. soil _____
12. roots _____

OPCIONES MÚLTIPLES

Marque con un círculo la letra de la respuesta correcta.

1. **shrubs**
   a. árboles
   b. hoyo
   c. arbustos
   d. hierbas

2. **branches**
   a. ramas
   b. hoyo
   c. hojas
   d. raíces

3. **clippings**
   a. flores
   b. plantas
   c. cortado
   d. zacate

4. **flowers**
   a. flores
   b. plantas
   c. cortado
   d. zacate

5. **hole**
   a. árboles
   b. hoyo
   c. arbustos
   d. hierbas

6. **branches**
   a. ramas
   b. hoyo
   c. hojas
   d. raíces

7. **trees**
   a. árboles
   b. hoyo
   c. arbustos
   d. hierbas

8. **leaves**
   a. ramas
   b. hoyo
   c. hojas
   d. raíces

9. **seeds**
   a. semillas
   b. raíces
   c. tierra
   d. zacate

10. **weeds**
    a. plantas
    b. hoyo
    c. arbustos
    d. hierbas

11. **roots**
    a. ramas
    b. hoyo
    c. hojas
    d. raíces

12. **soil**
    a. semillas
    b. raíces
    c. tierra
    d. zacate

PARTE II   TÉRMINOS DE ACCIÓN

Grupo 1		*Grupo 2*	
sopla	**blow**	poda	**prune**
excava	**dig**	rastrilla	**rake**
planta	**plant**	prepara	**prepare**
saca	**take out**	rocía	**spray**
instala	**install**	consigue	**get**
riega	**water**	muele	**mulch**

GRUPO 1 EJERCICIO DE CORRESPONDENCIA

Escriba la letra de la palabra en español junto a la palabra inglesa que corresponda a la izquierda.

1. _____ water   a. planta
2. _____ dig   b. instala
3. _____ plant   c. riega
4. _____ take out   d. sopla
5. _____ blow   e. excava
6. _____ install   f. saca

Traduzca al inglés.

1. instala _____
2. saca _____
3. planta _____
4. riega _____
5. sopla _____
6. excava _____

Traduzca al español.

1. water _____
2. plant _____
3. dig _____
4. install _____
5. take out _____
6. blow _____

GRUPO 2 EJERCICIO DE CORRESPONDENCIA

Escriba la letra de la palabra en español junto a la palabra inglesa que corresponda a la izquierda.

1. _____ prune   a. rocía
2. _____ rake   b. consigue
3. _____ prepare   c. muele
4. _____ get   d. poda
5. _____ spray   e. rastrilla
6. _____ mulch   f. prepara

Traduzca al inglés.

1. consigue _____
2. poda _____
3. rastrilla _____
4. muele _____
5. rocía _____
6. prepara _____

Traduzca al español.

1. mulch _____
2. prune _____
3. prepare _____
4. rake _____
5. get _____
6. spray _____

CRUCIGRAMAS

Horizontal

3. prune
6. get
7. plant
8. blow
9. water
10. mulch
11. dig

Vertical

1. spray
2. rake
3. prepare
4. take out
5. install

Horizontal

2. excava
5. rocía
6. planta
7. consigue
8. sopla
10. saca
11. poda

Vertical

1. prepara
3. instala
4. rastrilla
9. riega

OPCIONES MÚLTIPLES

Marque con un círculo la letra de la respuesta correcta.

1. **dig**
   a. consigue
   b. rocía
   c. riega
   d. excava

2. **blow**
   a. poda
   b. planta
   c. prepara
   d. sopla

3. **take out**
   a. instala
   b. saca
   c. mezcla
   d. muele

4. **get**
   a. consigue
   b. rocía
   c. riega
   d. excava

5. **plant**
   a. poda
   b. planta
   c. prepara
   d. sopla

6. **mulch**
   a. instala
   b. saca
   c. mezcla
   d. muele

7. **water**
   a. consigue
   b. rocía
   c. riega
   e. excava

8. **prune**
   a. poda
   b. planta
   c. prepara
   d. sopla

9. **spray**
   a. consigue
   b. rocía
   c. riega
   d. excava

10. **mix**
    a. instala
    b. saca
    c. mezcla
    d. muele

REPASO

Traduzca al inglés.

1. Riega las flores. _____
2. Prepara la tierra. _____
3. Sopla el cortado. _____
4. Rastrilla las hojas. _____
5. Planta las flores. _____
6. Instala los árboles. _____
7. Muele las plantas. _____
8. Saca las hierbas. _____
9. Poda las ramas. _____
10. Excava el hoyo. _____
11. Consigue las flores. _____
12. Rocía el zacate. _____

Traduzca al español.

1. Get the plants. _____
2. Dig the hole. _____
3. Take out the weeds. _____
4. Mulch the plants. _____
5. Prune the branches. _____
6. Water the shrubs. _____
7. Get the soil. _____
8. Rake the leaves. _____
9. Blow the clippings. _____
10. Prepare the soil. _____
11. Prune the trees. _____
12. Spray the grass. _____

LA GRAMÁTICA: ¿HAS TERMINADO?

Si su jefe le pregunta "*Did you. . .?*", él quiere saber si usted ha terminado una tarea del trabajo. "*Did you. . .?*" es similar en significado a las terminaciones *–aste* e *–iste* en español.

Plant**a**. . .   Plant. . .
¿Plant**aste**. . .?   Did you plant. . .?

Sopl**a**. . .   Blow. . .
¿Sopl**aste**. . .?   Did you blow. . .

Pod**a**. . .   Prune. . .
¿Pod**aste**. . .?   Did you prune. . .

Consig**ue**. . .   Get
¿Consig**uiste**. . .?   Did you get. . .

Muel**e**. . .   Mulch. . .
¿Mol**iste**. . .?   Did you mulch. . .

Lo siguente es la manera más facil contestar a tu jefe.

Sí, ya.	**Yes, I did.**
No.	**No, I did not. (No, I didn't.)**
No, todavia, no.	**No, not yet.**

EJERCICIO DE TRADUCCIÓN

Traduzca al inglés.

1. ¿Preparaste. . .? _____

2. ¿Podaste. . .? _____

3. ¿Plantaste. . .? _____

4. ¿Sacaste. . .? _____

5. ¿Instalaste. . .? _____

6. ¿Rociaste. . .? _____

7. ¿Conseguiste. . .? _____

8. ¿Moliste. . .? _____

Traduzca al español.

1. Did you plant the flowers? _____

2. Did you blow the leaves? _____

3. Did you dig the hole? _____

4. Did you install the trees? _____

5. Did you prune the branches? _____

6. Did you take out the weeds? _____

7. Did you spray the weeds? _____

8. Did you rake the leaves? _____

EJERCICIO ORAL

Did you. . .? Se acaba el día de trabajo y usted y su jefe van en un vehículo de regreso a la oficina. Pregunte y responda si se han realizado las tareas del trabajo. Sigue el modelo.

STUDENT A: Did you prune the branches?

STUDENT B: Yes, sir.

No, not yet.

poda

1. planta

2. sopla

3. consigue

4. poda

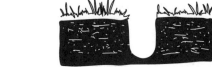

5. excava

6. saca

7. rastrilla

8. rocía

LA GRAMÁTICA: ACCIONES EN EL PASADO

Lo siguiente es una lista de acciones en el pasado. Muchas de las palabras terminen en 'ed' pero hay otras que son irregulares.

regué	**I watered**	No, no regué	**No, I didn't water**
planté	**I planted**	No, no planté	**No, I didn't plant**
mezclé	**I mixed**	No, no mezclé	**No, I didn't mix**
podé	**I pruned**	No, no podé	**No, I didn't prune**
rastrillé	**I raked**	No, no rastrillé	**No, I didn't rake**
rocié	**I sprayed**	No, no rocié	**No, I didn't spray**

REPASO

Lea el diálogo en voz alta en inglés. Seguidamente tradúzcalo al español.

Jack: Hello Miguel. How's it going?

Miguel: Good morning, boss!

Jack: I'd like to introduce you to Alejandro.

Miguel: Nice to meet you.

Alejandro: Same to you.

Miguel: From where are you, Alejandro?

Alejandro: I'm from Aguascalientes, Mexico.

Miguel: I'm from Guatemala. I'm Guatemalan.

Jack: Miguel . . . go to the apartments.

Miguel: Okay.

Jack: Plant the trees.

Miguel: And the flowers?

Jack: Yes. Water the trees and the flowers.

Miguel: And cut the grass?

Jack: Yes . . . and please . . . take out the weeds.

Miguel: Take out the roots . . . yes, yes. . .

Jack: Thank you. You're a hard worker!

(later that afternoon)

Jack: How's it going, Miguel?

Miguel: Fine . . . perfect.

Jack: Are there problems?

Miguel: Ah . . . I am worried.

Lea el diálogo en voz alta en español. Seguidamente tradúzcalo al inglés.

Jack: Hola Miguel. ¿Qué tal?

Miguel: ¡Buenos días, jefe!

Jack: Quiero presentarte a Alejandro.

Miguel: Mucho gusto.

Alejandro: Igualmente.

Miguel: ¿De dónde eres, Alejandro?

Alejandro: Soy de Aguascalientes, México.

Miguel: Soy de Guatemala. Soy guatamalteco.

Jack: Miguel . . . vete a los apartamentos.

Miguel: Está bién.

Jack: Planta los árboles.

Miguel: ¿Y las flores?

Jack: Sí. Riega los árboles y las flores.

Miguel: ¿Y corta el zacate?

Jack: Sí . . . y por favor . . . saca las hierbas.

Miguel: Saca las raíces . . . sí, sí . . .

Jack: Gracias. ¡Eres muy trabajador!

(Más tarde, por la tarde)

Jack: ¿Qué tal, Miguel?

Miguel: Bien . . . perfecto.

Jack: ¿Hay problemas?

Miguel: Ah . . . Estoy preocupado.

Jack:	Why?	**Jack:**	¿Por qué?
Miguel:	Ah . . . The woman is furious!	**Miguel:**	Ah . . . ¡La mujer está furiosa!
Jack:	Why?	**Jack:**	¿Por qué?
Jack:	Did you plant the trees?	**Jack:**	¿Plantaste los árboles?
Miguel:	Yes, boss. And the flowers.	**Miguel:**	Sí, jefe. Y las flores.
Jack:	Did you prune the shrubs?	**Jack:**	¿Podaste los arbustos?
Miguel:	Yes, sir.	**Miguel:**	Sí, señor.
Jack:	Hmmm . . .	**Jack:**	Hmmm . . .
Miguel:	Come with me, Jack. There is a lot of water . . .	**Miguel:**	Ven conmigo, Jack. Hay mucha agua . . .
Jack:	Oh, no! Yes . . . The woman is in a bad mood!	**Jack:**	Oh, no! ¡Sí . . . La mujer está de mal humor!

Traduzca al español.

1. I'm studying Spanish. _____

2. Do you speak English? _____

3. It's good. It's bad. It's correct. _____

4. Everything else is perfect. _____

5. Incredible! You're very strong! _____

6. Who is the manager? _____

7. Where is the foreman? _____

8. There are seven days in a week. _____

9. I like the summer. I swim. I fish. _____

10. Do you swim? Do you fish? _____

11. Does your ankle hurt? _____

12. Where is the first aid kit? _____

13. Give me the pruner. _____

14. Load the blowers. _____

15. Mix the oil and gas. _____

LA CULTURA: CÓMO LA HISTORIA DE UN PAÍS AFECTA A LA CONDUCTA DE SUS CIUDADANOS

Hay muchas diferencias entre los Estados Unidos y los países latinoamericanos en sus valores, formas de conducta y estilos de vida. Estas diferencias afectan la forma cómo se realizan los negocios. Una comparación de la historia de cada país nos explica porqué estas culturas son tan diferentes hoy en día.

Todos los alumnos de secundaria en los Estados Unidos estudian la materia "Historia de los Estados Unidos." Para aprobar los exámenes, memorizan las fechas de las batallas *ganadas,* los territorios *añadidos* a su nación o algunas otras conquistas *positivas.* A mediados del siglo XIX, Méjico decidió no vender sus tierras a los Estados Unidos y por esa razón los mejicanos tuvieron que luchar por esas tierras. En los Estados Unidos, las expresiones históricas populares eran "¡Conquistamos el Oeste!" y "¡Construímos América!" Incluso hoy en día, los ciudadanos de Estados Unidos piensan muy poco en las cosas perdidas y los fracasos.

A raíz de su pasado, los ciudadanos de los Estados Unidos se consideran positivos, optimistas, con confianza en sí mismos y en su capacidad para ser líderes competentes. No temen los desafíos. Es aventureros dispuestos a correr riesgos. Quieren cambiar las cosas, mejorarlas, perfeccionarlas, para hacerlas más rápidas, más resistentes y más seguras. Tienen la mentalidad de progreso.

La historia mejicana es diferente. Es un pueblo conquistado. En el siglo XVI, el español Hernán Cortés y su pequeña banda de soldados completaron la Conquista en menos de dos años, extendiendo el dominio español hacia el sur por Centroamérica llegando incluso hasta Alaska por el Norte. España gobernó en Méjico durante los trescientos años siguientes. En el siglo XIX, Maximiliano y los franceses llegaron a gobernar en Méjico. Luego, en 1846 se desencadenó la guerra entre Méjico y Estados Unidos y los mexicanos perdieron más de la mitad de su territorio ante unos Estados Unidos llenos de confianza. Fue un acontecimiento monumental y una derrota devastadora.

Esta presencia continua de un grupo dominante hizo que algunas culturas latinas piensen que la gente de piel blanca es superior a los demás. Esto les creó un sentido de inferioridad. Algunos latinos piensan que los conquistadores españoles deliberadamente crearon una clase inferior oprimida con una mentalidad arraigada en la pasividad y el fracaso. El concepto de autoridad se ha convertido en la norma.

En los Estados Unidos, "Todos los hombres se crearon iguales." En los países latinoamericanos, las diferencias ciertamente marcan la diferencia. Se trata de una sociedad muy jerarquizada. La edad, el sexo, las funciones que se ejercen y la posición social que se ocupa son extremadamente importantes.

9

Las Materiales y Los Recipientes

PARTE I   LAS MATERIALES

el fertilizante
fertilizer

la turba
peat moss

la tierra
soil

la corteza
bark

la paja
pine straw

la mezcla
mulch (mixture)

la arena
sand

el abono
compost

las semillas
seeds

los ladrillos
bricks

las piedras
stones

la roca
rock

el zacate
sod

el cemento
cement

el barro
clay

EJERCICIO DE CORRESPONDENCIA

Escriba la letra de cada dibujo al lado de la palabra inglesa que corresponda abajo.

a.

b. PINE STRAW

c. SOIL

d. BARK

e. FERTILIZER

f. MULCH

g.

h. COMPOST

i. SEEDS

j. PEAT MOSS

k. STONES

l.

1. _____ soil
2. _____ bark
3. _____ pine straw
4. _____ mulch
5. _____ fertilizer
6. _____ peat moss

7. _____ seeds
8. _____ sand
9. _____ compost
10. _____ stones
11. _____ rock
12. _____ bricks

EJERCICIO DE VOCABULARIO

Escriba la palabra inglesa abajo.

1. _____   2. _____   3. _____   4. _____

5. _____   6. _____   7. _____   8. _____

9. _____   10. _____   11. _____   12. _____

EJERCICIO DE CORRESPONDENCIA

Escriba la letra de la palabra en español junto a la palabra inglesa que corresponda a la izquierda.

1. _____ sand
2. _____ compost
3. _____ seeds
4. _____ bricks
5. _____ fertilizer
6. _____ peat moss
7. _____ soil
8. _____ bark

9. _____ pine straw
10. _____ mulch
11. _____ sod
12. _____ cement
13. _____ clay
14. _____ stones
15. _____ rock

a. la mezcla
b. la paja
c. la roca
d. la tierra
e. el fertilizante
f. la turba
g. el zacate
h. la corteza

i. el cemento
j. la arena
k. el abono
l. las semillas
m. el barro
n. las piedras
o. los ladrillos

CRUCIGRAMAS

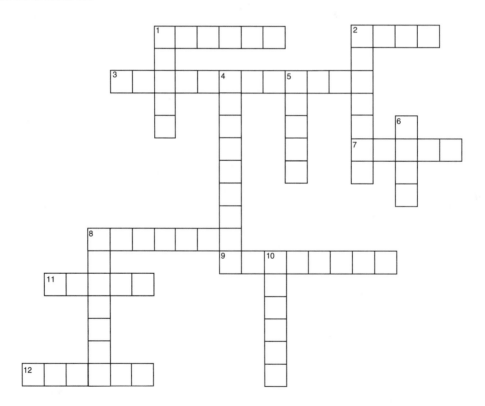

Horizontal

1. soil
2. pine straw
3. fertilizer
7. compost
8. cement
9. seeds
11. clay
12. sod

Vertical

1. peat moss
2. stones
4. bricks
5. sand
6. rock
8. bark
10. mulch

Horizontal

1. roca
5. turba
7. paja
8. mezcla
9. zacate
11. ladrillos
15. tierra

Vertical

2. abono
3. fertilizante
4. arena
6. semillas
10. corteza
12. cemento
13. piedras
14. barro

EJERCICIO DE TRADUCCIÓN

Traduzca al inglés.

1. los ladrillos _____

2. las piedras _____

3. la roca _____

4. la paja _____

5. la mezcla _____

6. la arena _____

7. el abono _____

8. las semillas _____

9. el zacate _____

10. el cemento _____

11. el barro _____

12. el fertilizante _____

13. la turba _____

14. la tierra _____

15. la corteza _____

Traduzca al español.

1. seeds _____

2. bricks _____

3. fertilizer _____

4. peat moss _____

5. pine straw _____

6. mulch _____

7. sand _____

8. soil _____

9. bark _____

10. compost _____

11. stones _____

12. cement _____

13. clay _____

14. rock _____

15. sod _____

OPCIONES MÚLTIPLES

Marque con un círculo la letra de la respuesta correcta.

1. sand
   a. la turba
   b. la tierra
   c. la corteza
   d. la arena

2. compost
   a. el abono
   b. el fertilizante
   c. la arena
   d. el zacate

3. seeds
   a. las piedras
   b. las semillas
   c. los ladrillos
   d. la mezcla

4. stones
   a. las piedras
   b. las semillas
   c. los ladrillos
   d. la mezcla

5. rock
   a. la paja
   b. la roca
   c. la corteza
   d. la turba

6. sod
   a. la turba
   b. los ladrillos
   c. la tierra
   d. el zacate

7. bricks
   a. el cemento
   b. las piedras
   c. las semillas
   d. los ladrillos

8. peat moss
   a. la paja
   b. la roca
   c. la corteza
   d. la turba

9. soil
   a. la tierra
   b. la arena
   c. el barro
   d. la turba

10. bark
   a. la paja
   b. la roca
   c. la corteza
   d. la turba

11. pine straw
   a. la paja
   b. la roca
   c. la corteza
   d. la turba

12. mulch
   a. el abono
   b. la fertilizante
   c. el zacate
   d. la mezcla

PARTE II   LOS RECIPIENTES

el saco	**bag**
la paleta	**pallet**
la maceta (de plástico, de barro)	**pot (plastic, clay)**
la lata	**can**
el montón	**pile**
la caja	**box**
la carretilla	**wheelbarrow**
el baúl	**car trunk**

Medidas

pulgadas	**inches**
pies	**feet**
yardas	**yards**
galones	**gallons**
una pulgada	**1 inch**
dos pulgadas	**2 inches**
un pie	**1 foot**
dos pies	**2 feet**
dos por tres	**2 by 3**
media yarda	**1/2 yard**
una yarda	**1 yard**
dos yardas	**2 yards**
un galón	**1 gallon**
dos galones	**2 gallons**
tres galones	**3 gallons**
cinco galones	**5 gallons**
quince galones	**15 gallons**
veinte y cinco galones	**25 gallons**

EJERCICIO DE CORRESPONDENCIA

Escriba la letra de la palabra en español junto a la palabra inglesa que corresponda a la izquierda.

1. _____ pot	7. _____ pallet	a. la lata	g. los pies
2. _____ bag	8. _____ pile	b. las yardas	h. la caja
3. _____ car trunk	9. _____ box	c. la carretilla	i. el montón
4. _____ inches	10. _____ wheelbarrow	d. la maceta	j. el baúl
5. _____ feet	11. _____ can	e. los galones	k. la paleta
6. _____ gallons	12. _____ yards	f. las pulgadas	l. el saco

CRUCIGRAMAS

Horizontal

3. gallons
4. pallet
6. can
7. car trunk
8. bag
9. feet
10. wheelbarrow

Vertical

1. yards
2. box
4. inches
5. pot

Horizontal

4. montón
5. pies
7. baúl
8. caja
9. galónes

Vertical

1. pulgadas
2. carretilla
3. paleta
4. maceta
6. lata
8. saco

EJERCICIO DE TRADUCCIÓN

Traduzca al inglés.

1. las pulgadas _____
2. los pies _____
3. la carretilla _____
4. los galones _____
5. la paleta _____
6. el montón _____
7. la maceta _____
8. el saco _____
9. el baúl _____
10. la lata _____
11. las yardas _____
12. la caja _____

Traduzca al español.

1. pot _____
2. bag _____
3. car trunk _____
4. inches _____
5. feet _____
6. gallons _____
7. pallet _____
8. pile _____
9. box _____
10. wheelbarrow _____
11. can _____
12. yards _____

OPCIONES MÚLTIPLES

Marque con un círculo la letra de la respuesta correcta.

1. **pot**
   a. la paleta
   b. la lata
   c. la maceta
   d. la caja

2. **bag**
   a. el saco
   b. el baúl
   c. la carretilla
   d. el montón

3. **inches**
   a. las yardas
   b. las pulgadas
   c. los galones
   d. los pies

4. **car trunk**
   a. el saco
   b. el baúl
   c. la carretilla
   d. el montón

5. **feet**
   a. las yardas
   b. las pulgadas
   c. los galones
   d. los pies

6. **gallons**
   a. las yardas
   b. las pulgadas
   c. los galones
   d. los pies

7. **pallet**
   a. la paleta
   b. la lata
   c. la maceta
   d. la caja

8. **pile**
   a. el saco
   b. el baúl
   c. la carretilla
   d. el montón

9. **box**
   a. la paleta
   b. la lata
   c. la maceta
   d. la caja

10. **wheelbarrow**
    a. el saco
    b. el baúl
    c. la carretilla
    d. el montón

11. **can**
    a. la paleta
    b. la lata
    c. la maceta
    d. la caja

12. **yards**
    a. las yardas
    b. las pulgadas
    c. los galones
    d. los pies

PARTE III   TÉRMINOS DE ACCIÓN

Grupo 1		*Grupo 2*	
aplica	**apply**	añade	**add**
rastrilla	**rake**	barre	**sweep**
carga	**load**	consigue	**get**
descarga	**unload**	cepilla	**brush**
saca	**take out**	pisa	**tamp**
empareja	**spread**	pon	**put**

GRUPO 1

Ejercicio de Correspondencia

Escriba la letra de la palabra en español junto a la palabra inglesa que corresponda a la izquierda.

1. _____ unload
2. _____ take out
3. _____ spread
4. _____ apply
5. _____ rake
6. _____ load

a. carga
b. saca
c. empareja
d. rastrilla
e. descarga
f. aplica

Traduzca al inglés.

1. empareja _____
2. aplica _____
3. rastrilla _____
4. carga _____
5. saca _____
6. descarga _____

Traduzca al español.

1. rake _____
2. apply _____
3. unload _____
4. take out _____
5. spread _____
6. load _____

GRUPO 2

Ejercicio de Correspondencia

Escriba la letra de la palabra en español junto a la palabra inglesa que corresponda a la izquierda.

1. _____ get
2. _____ brush
3. _____ tamp
4. _____ add
5. _____ sweep
6. _____ put

a. pisa
b. consigue
c. barre
d. cepilla
e. pon
f. añade

Traduzca al inglés.

1. pisa _____
2. pon _____
3. añade _____
4. barre _____
5. consigue _____
6. cepilla _____

Traduzca al español.

1. put _____
2. add _____
3. get _____
4. brush _____
5. tamp _____
6. sweep _____

CRUCIGRAMAS

Horizontal

1. put
2. load
4. take out
6. sweep
7. brush
9. spread
10. apply
11. get

Vertical

1. tamp
3. rake
5. add
8. unload

Horizontal

3. pon
4. carga
5. consigue
7. aplica
8. añade
10. descarga
11. pisa

Vertical

1. empareja
2. rastrilla
6. saca
9. cepilla

OPCIONES MÚLTIPLES

Marque con un círculo la letra de la respuesta correcta.

1. **take out**
   a. pisa
   b. saca
   c. aplica
   d. pon

2. **add**
   a. barre
   b. descarga
   c. carga
   d. añade

3. **spread**
   a. rastrilla
   b. empareja
   c. pisa
   d. cepilla

4. **sweep**
   a. barre
   b. descarga
   c. carga
   d. añade

5. **get**
   a. cepilla
   b. consigue
   c. carga
   d. pisa

6. **apply**
   a. pisa
   b. saca
   c. aplica
   d. pon

7. **rake**
   a. rastrilla
   b. empareja
   c. pisa
   d. cepilla

8. **load**
   a. añade
   b. aplica
   c. carga
   d. barre

9. **brush**
   a. rastrilla
   b. empareja
   c. pisa
   d. cepilla

10. **tamp**
    a. pisa
    b. saca
    c. aplica
    d. pon

LA GRAMÁTICA

Para expresar que una persona realiza una acción, añada una "*s*" o la terminación "*es*" a la palabra que describe la acción.

Juan carga las rastrillas.	Juan loads the rakes.
Mike consigue la gasolina.	Pablo gets the gas.
Pilar usa la escoba.	Pilar uses the broom.
Sue lava la carretilla.	Sue washes the wheelbarrow.

Traduzca al inglés.

1. Pablo descarga. . . _____

2. Marcos usa. . . _____

3. Juan pone. . . _____

4. Mary carga. . . _____

5. Javier consigue. . . _____

6. Ana limpia. . . _____

7. Carlos lava. . . _____

8. Paco mezcla. . . _____

LA GRAMÁTICA: ÉL Y ELLA

él	**he**
ella	**she**

En los capítulos anteriores, aprendío usted cómo asignar y comprender las tareas usando la forma del manda miento. Ha aprendido hablar directa mente a una persona. Ahora, usando la misma forma de la palabra usted puede hablar acerca de una persona. Estudie los ejemplos siguientes.

Hablando directamente a una persona:

Hola, Raúl! Por favor. . . planta las flores.   **Hi, Raúl! Please. . . plant the flowers.**
Gracias.   **Thanks.**

Hablando de una persona:

Raúl planta las flores.   **Raúl plants (is planting) the flowers.**

EJERCICIO ORAL

¿Qué hace Miguel? Trabaje con un compañero. Pregunte y responda: *What is Miguel doing?* Sigue el modelo.

STUDENT A:	What is Miguel doing?
STUDENT B:	Miguel loads (is loading) the soil.

carga

1. rastrilla

5. carga

2. empareja

6. descarga

3. añade

7. saca

4. barre

8. spread

REPASO

Traduzca al inglés.

1. Paco, carga las piedras, por favor. _____

2. José carga las piedras. _____

3. Rosa, pisa la tierra, por favor. _____

4. Ana pisa la tierra. _____

5. Alberto, descarga los ladrillos, por favor. _____

6. Javier descarga los ladrillos. _____

7. María, consigue la turba, por favor. _____

8. Antonio saca el barro. _____

9. Paco, añade más mezcla, por favor. _____

10. Jesus rastrilla la arena. _____

Traduzca al español.

1. Paco, load the stones, please. _____

2. Javier loads the stones. _____

3. Juan, get the fertilizer, please. _____

4. Carlos gets the fertilizer. _____

5. Pilar, spread out the soil, please. _____

6. Teresa spreads out the soil. _____

7. Antono, add more mulch, please. _____

8. Ana, get the pine straw, please. _____

9. Susana spreads the pine straw. _____

10. Jesus gets the peat moss. _____

Lea el cuento en voz alta en inglés. Seguidamente tradúzcalo al español.

Jim is the boss of the Green Landscapes Company, Inc. Jim works a lot in the months of March, April, May, June and July. Jim is very responsible. Jim works a lot in the office and with the clients. Jim is the manager of the region.

Jack works a lot. Jack supervises many Latinos. . .three crews. Jack studies Spanish and his teacher is very patient and organized. Her name is Kathy. Jack practices Spanish a lot with Kathy and the crews.

The Latinos are very cooperative and hard working.

Miguel is from Guadalajara, Mexico. Miguel is the foreman of the crew. He is thirty two years old. Domingo, Paco and Berto are brothers. Miguel is their uncle. Domingo cuts the grass. Domingo takes out the weeds and pulls the roots. Paco blows the leaves while* Berto rakes the leaves. Domingo prunes the shrubs. Miguel plants and waters the flowers.

In the afternoon,** Jack studies Spanish vocabulary a lot. Jack practices with Miguel. Jack and Miguel know that*** communication equals**** productivity.

    * while – mientras
   ** In the afternoon – Por la tarde
  *** know that – saben que
**** equal – es igual a

Lea el cuento en voz alta en español. Seguidamente tradúzcalo al inglés.

Jim es el jefe de la compañia Green Landscapes, Inc. Jim trabaja mucho en los meses de marzo, abril, mayo, junio y julio. Jim es muy responsible. Jim trabaja mucho en la oficina y con los clientes. Es el gerente de la región.

Jack trabaja mucho. Jack supervisa a muchos latinos. . . tres cuadrillas. Jack estudia español y su profesora es muy paciente y organizada. Se llama Kathy. Jack practica el español mucho con Kathy y con las cuadrillas.

Los latinos son muy cooperativos y trabajadores.

Miguel es de Guadalajara, Méjico. Miguel es el mayordomo de la cuadrilla. Tiene treinta y dos años. Domingo, Paco y Berto son hermanos. Miguel es su tío. Domingo corta el zacate. Domingo saca las hierbas y jala las raíces. Paco sopla las hojas mientras* Berto rastrilla las hojas. Domingo poda los arbustos. Miguel planta y riega las flores.

Por la tarde,** Jack estudia mucho el vocabulario español. Jack practica con Miguel. Jack y Miguel saben que*** la comunicación es igual a**** la productividad.

    * mientras – while
   ** Por la tarde – In the afternoon
  *** saben que – They know that
**** es igual a – equals

Traduzca al español.

1. How's your family? _____

2. Carlos is from Honduras. He's Honduran. _____

3. Help me. Watch me. _____

4. Try it. Keep trying. _____

5. How many? When? Where? _____

6. What time is it? _____

7. I'm angry. I'm tired. I'm sick. _____

8. What's your wife's name? _____

9. What's your daughter's name? _____

10. How old is your son? _____

11. Do you like to play volleyball? _____

12. I like to play cards. Do you play cards? _____

13. Get the wheelbarrow. _____

14. Load the blowers and the rakes. _____

15. Wear the safety glasses, gloves, and boots. _____

LA CULTURA: DIRIGIR Y SUPERVISAR

Uno de los factores más significativos y problemáticos relacionados con el trabajo consiste en la forma como la gente trata sus diferencias y cómo interactúan los supervisores y sus subordinados. Las culturas difieren en la forma como ven la edad, el sexo, las funciones y la posición social de una persona. En los Estados Unidos, la gente tiende a restarle importancia a tales factores, pero en las culturas latinoamericanas, esas diferencias son esenciales y muy significativas.

Los latinos tienen un gran respeto por la autoridad. Tradicionalmente, los jóvenes empleados latinos nunca dudan o ni siquiera comentan una decisión que su superior haya tomado, incluso si están completamente en desacuerdo con esa decisión. Tampoco los supervisores latinos aceptan normalmente ningún cuestionamiento de parte de sus subordinados. En los países latinoamericanos no autoridad; esa idea es ajena a la mayoría de la gente. El supervisor conserva el poder y las cuestiones de importancia se deciden entre los jefes. Los subordinados no actúan enérgicamente con previsión de futuro sino que esperan instrucciones específicas. La mayoría de los subordinados prefieren este método, puesto que los libera de la posibilidad de cometer errores y quedar mal. Muchas veces los subordinados se sienten inseguros y temen cometer errores. Sin embargo, es importante señalar que está surgiendo una nueva generación de supervisores latinos que, como resultado de la educación universitaria, respaldan firmemente la costumbre de delegar responsabilidades.

En los Estados Unidos, se cría a los niños para que sean independientes y deseen tomar sus propias decisiones. Y por esa razón, los jóvenes empleados estadounidenses normalmente son reacios a pedir consejos. Quieren tener tanta responsabilidad y autoridad como sea posible. El hecho de que se ejerza autoridad sobre ellos les desagrada y no les gusta tener que pedir la aprobación para cada decisión y cada acto que se propongan realizar. Se sienten capaces y quieren que se les permita tomar la mayoría de las decisiones por sí mismos.

Ellos prosperan enfrentándose a nuevos problemas sin ayuda. Sienten seguridad en sus apreciaciones y saben muy bien que un pequeño error no les hará perder el respeto y el apoyo de sus supervisores, porque cometer un pequeño error al comienzo se considera como algo normal en el proceso de aprendizaje.

10

El Vivero

PARTE I   EL VIVERO

el sol
sun

la sombra
shade

las etiquetas
tags, labels

los precios
prices

los nombres
names

las anuales
annuals

las perennes
perennials

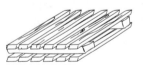

la paleta
pallet

las canastas colgadas
hanging baskets

la maceta
pot

el carrito
cart

el flat
flat

el recipiente
container

la mesa de plantar
potting bench

145

EJERCICIO DE CORRESPONDENCIA

Escriba la letra de cada dibujo al lado de la palabra inglesa que corresponda abajo.

a.

b.

c.

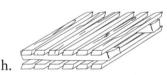

d.

e.

f.

g.

h.

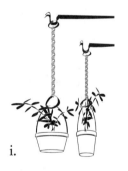

i.

j.

k.

l.

1. _____ prices

2. _____ pot

3. _____ annuals

4. _____ perennials

5. _____ names

6. _____ labels

7. _____ hanging baskets

8. _____ pallet

9. _____ shade

10. _____ container

11. _____ cart

12. _____ sun

EJERCICIO DE VOCABULARIO

Escriba la palabra inglesa abajo.

1. _____

2. _____

3. _____

4. _____

5. _____

6. _____

7. _____

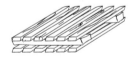

8. _____

9. _____

10. _____

11. _____

12. _____

EJERCICIO DE CORRESPONDENCIA

Escriba la letra de la palabra en español junto al la palabra inglesa que corresponda a la izquierda.

1. _____ tags, labels
2. _____ prices
3. _____ names
4. _____ annuals
5. _____ perennials
6. _____ pallet
7. _____ hanging baskets
8. _____ pot

9. _____ cart
10. _____ flat
11. _____ container
12. _____ potting bench
13. _____ sun
14. _____ shade
15. _____ plants

a. el carrito
b. los perennes
c. la mesa de plantar
d. la sombra
e. los precios
f. el recipiente
g. la maceta

h. las canastas colgadas
i. el flat
j. las etiquetas
k. la paleta
l. las plantas
m. las anuales
n. el sol
o. los nombres

Horizontal

1. prices
5. cart
6. pallet
8. names
9. shade
11. plants
12. perennials
14. flat
15. container

Vertical

2. tags, labels
3. sun
4. pot
7. annuals
10. hanging baskets
13. potting bench

Horizontal

4. plantas
8. carrito
9. flat
10. sombra
11. nombres
12. perennes
13. recipiente
14. maceta

Vertical

1. mesa de plantar
2. sol
3. anuales
4. precios
5. etiquetas
6. canastas colgadas
7. paleta

EJERCICIO DE TRADUCCIÓN

Traduzca al inglés.

1. el carrito _____

2. los perennes _____

3. la mesa de plantar _____

4. el sol _____

5. los precios _____

6. el recipiente _____

7. la maceta _____

8. las canastas colgadas _____

9. el flat _____

10. las etiquetas _____

11. la paleta _____

12. las plantas _____

13. las anuales _____

14. la sombra _____

15. los nombres _____

Traduzca al español.

1. annuals _____

2. perennials _____

3. pallet _____

4. tags, labels _____

5. prices _____

6. names _____

7. hanging baskets _____

8. pot _____

9. shade _____

10. sun _____

11. plants _____

12. cart _____

13. flat _____

14. container _____

15. potting bench _____

OPCIONES MÚLTIPLES

Marque con un círculo la letra de la respuesta correcta.

1. **potting bench**
   a. el carrito
   b. la maceta
   c. la mesa de plantar
   d. la sombra

2. **pallet**
   a. los precios
   b. la paleta
   c. la maceta
   d. las etiquetas

3. **prices**
   a. los precios
   b. la paleta
   c. las plantas
   d. las etiquetas

4. **shade**
   a. las anuales
   b. los precios

   c. la sombra
   d. las plantas

5. **cart**
   a. los perennes
   b. la mesa de plantar
   c. las macetas
   d. el carrito

6. **container**
   a. el recipiente
   b. la maceta
   c. el flat
   d. la paleta

7. **hanging baskets**
   a. las anuales
   b. los precios
   c. las canastas colgadas
   d. la mesa de plantar

8. **tags, labels**
   a. los precios
   b. los nombres
   c. las plantas
   d. las etiquetas

9. **pot**
   a. los precios
   b. la maceta
   c. la paleta
   d. el flat

10. **perennials**
    a. los perennes
    b. la paleta
    c. las plantas
    d. los precios

PARTE II TÉRMINOS DE ACCIÓN

Grupo 1		Grupo 2	
planta	**pot**	saca	**dig up**
replanta	**repot**	deshierba	**weed**
corta la mala	**deadhead**	pon	**put, tag**
prepara	**prepare**	haz bola	**ball**
mueve	**move**	pon en costal	**burlap**
consigue	**get**	carga	**load**
envuelve	**wrap**	descarga	**unload**

GRUPO 1

Ejercicio de Correspondencia

Escriba la letra de la palabra en español junto a la palabra inglesa que corresponda a la izquierda.

1. _____ deadhead
2. _____ pot
3. _____ prepare
4. _____ move
5. _____ repot
6. _____ get
7. _____ wrap

a. replanta
b. envuelve
c. consigue
d. planta
e. corta la mala
f. prepara
g. mueve

Traduzca al inglés.

1. prepara _____
2. mueve _____
3. consigue _____
4. corta la mala _____
5. planta _____
6. replanta _____
7. envuelve _____

Traduzca al español.

1. deadhead _____
2. move _____
3. get _____
4. repot _____
5. wrap _____
6. pot _____
7. prepare _____

GRUPO 2

Ejercicio de Correspondencia

Escriba la letra de la palabra en español junto a la palabra inglesa que corresponda a la izquierda.

1. _____ dig up   a. descarga
2. _____ put, tag   b. carga
3. _____ unload   c. pon
4. _____ ball   d. deshierba
5. _____ burlap   e. pon en costal
6. _____ load   f. saca
7. _____ weed   g. haz bola

Traduzca al inglés.

1. pon _____

2. haz bola _____

3. descarga _____

4. deshierba _____

5. saca _____

6. pon en costal _____

7. carga _____

Traduzca al español.

1. weed _____

2. ball _____

3. burlap _____

4. dig up _____

5. load _____

6. put, tag _____

7. unload _____

CRUCIGRAMAS

Horizontal

3. put, tag
5. move
6. get
8. ball
9. weed
11. pot
12. dig up

Vertical

1. repot
2. wrap
4. burlap
6. deadhead
7. load
9. unload
10. prepare

Horizontal

3. replanta
4. consigue
6. carga
7. deshierba
9. haz bola
11. descarga

Vertical

1. corta la mala
2. planta
5. mueve
7. envuelve
8. saca
9. pon en costal
10. pon

OPCIONES MÚLTIPLES

Marque con un círculo la letra de la respuesta correcta.

1. **move**
   a. carga
   b. saca
   c. mueve
   d. envuelve

2. **get**
   a. consigue
   b. carga
   c. mueve
   d. pon

3. **prepare**
   a. pon en costal
   b. planta
   c. pon
   d. prepara

4. **wrap**
   a. mueve
   b. envuelve
   c. haz bola
   d. pon en costal

5. **dig up**
   a. carga
   b. descarga
   c. saca
   d. deshierba

6. **pot**
   a. replanta
   b. planta
   c. saca
   d. carga

7. **ball**
   a. haz bola
   b. deshierba
   c. pon en costal
   d. corta la mala

8. **burlap**
   a. prepara
   b. envuelve
   c. haz bola
   d. pon en costal

9. **load**
   a. mueve
   b. consigue
   c. descarga
   d. carga

10. **repot**
    a. replanta
    b. prepara
    c. pon
    d. planta

11. **deadhead**
    a. pon
    b. mueve
    c. deshierba
    d. corta la mala

12. **weed**
    a. saca
    b. deshierba
    c. corta la mala
    d. pon

13. **put, tag**
    a. saca
    b. carga
    c. planta
    d. pon

14. **unload**
    a. descarga
    b. saca
    c. carga
    d. mueve

EJERCICIO ORAL

¡Llegó la primavera! ¡Su vivero se está preparando para la nueva ola primaveral de compras! Su compañero de trabajo le pregunta qué quiere usted que él etiquete. Seleccione su respuesta de los siguientes materiales. Sigue el modelo.

STUDENT A: What do you want?
               What would you like?

STUDENT B: Put the prices on the plants.

PARTE III   LOS COLORES

rojo	**red**	anaranjado	**orange**
blanco	**white**	rosado	**pink**
azul	**blue**	black	**negro**
verde	**green**	café	**brown**
morado	**purple**	gris	**grey**
amarillo	**yellow**		

EJERCICIO DE CORRESPONDENCIA

Escriba la letra de la palabra en español junto a la palabra inglesa que corresponda a la izquierda.

1. _____ black
2. _____ brown
3. _____ red
4. _____ white
5. _____ green
6. _____ blue
7. _____ grey
8. _____ pink
9. _____ orange
10. _____ yellow
11. _____ purple

a. blanco
b. negro
c. café
d. anaranjado
e. verde
f. gris
g. azul
h. rosado
i. rojo
j. morado
k. amarillo

CRUCIGRAMAS

Horizontal

3. yellow
4. brown
6. grey
8. black
9. white
10. purple

Vertical

1. green
2. pink
3. orange
5. blue
7. red

Horizontal

2. morado
5. verde
6. amarillo
9. café
10. rojo

Vertical

1. azul
2. rosado
3. anaranjado
4. negro
7. blanco
8. gris

EJERCICIO DE TRADUCCIÓN

Traduzca al inglés.

1. verde _____
2. amarillo _____
3. rojo _____
4. blanco _____
5. azul _____
6. anaranjado _____
7. rosado _____
8. negro _____
9. morado _____
10. café _____
11. gris _____

Traduzca al español.

1. blue _____
2. green _____
3. red _____
4. white _____
5. purple _____
6. grey _____
7. yellow _____
8. orange _____
9. black _____
10. brown _____
11. pink _____

OPCIONES MÚLTIPLES

Marque con un círculo la letra de la respuesta correcta.

1. pink
   a. anaranjado
   b. rosado
   c. rojo
   d. morado

2. green
   a. gris
   b. azul
   c. verde
   d. blanco

3. purple
   a. anaranjado
   b. morado
   c. azul
   d. amarillo

4. red
   a. rosado
   b. blanco

   c. café
   d. rojo

5. yellow
   a. rojo
   b. verde
   c. anaranjado
   d. amarillo

6. blue
   a. morado
   b. gris
   c. azul
   d. verde

7. white
   a. blanco
   b. azul
   c. morado
   d. negro

8. black
   a. blanco
   b. azul
   c. morado
   d. negro

9. orange
   a. anaranjado
   b. rosado
   c. rojo
   d. morado

10. brown
   a. negro
   b. blanco
   c. gris
   d. café

LA GRAMÁTICA: PALABRAS GRAMATICALES DESCRIPTIVAS

Al describir las cosas en inglés, la palabra descriptiva (el color, en este caso) se pone antes de la palabra.

las plantas rojas   the **red** plants
los arbustos blancos   the **white** shrubs

EJERCICIO DE TRADUCCIÓN

Traduzca al español.

1. the orange pots _____

2. the pink tags _____

3. the white perennials _____

4. the red annuals _____

5. the blue flats _____

6. the brown containers _____

7. the purple plants _____

8. the green trees _____

9. the yellow shrubs _____

10. the red hanging baskets _____

LA GRAMÁTICA: DESEOS

Para expresar preferencias y deseos en inglés, usamos la palabra. . .*Want*.

¿Quieres. . .?	**Do you want. . .?**
¿Qué quieres?	**What do you want?**
Quiero. . .	**I want. . .**
Querria. . .	**I would like. . .**

EJERCICIO ORAL

¡Ustedes consiguieron el contrato! ¡Imagínese que el diseño de su compañía fue seleccionado para la nueva urbanización en la ciudad! Usted está en el vivero comprando sus materiales. Trabaje con un compañero preguntando y respondiendo qué es lo que quiere y cuántas cosas quiere. Sigue el modelo.

STUDENT A:	What would you like, sir?
STUDENT B:	I would like the red shrubs.
STUDENT A:	How many?
STUDENT B:	Nine, please.

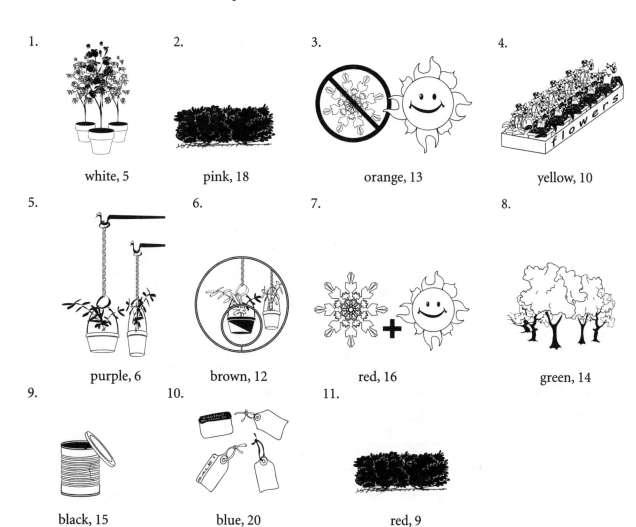

1. white, 5
2. pink, 18
3. orange, 13
4. yellow, 10

5. purple, 6
6. brown, 12
7. red, 16
8. green, 14

9. black, 15
10. blue, 20
11. red, 9

EJERCICIO DE TRADUCCIÓN

Traduzca al inglés.

1. ¿Qué quieres? _____

2. Quiero tres canastas colgadas rojas. _____

3. Quiero cinco macetas anaranjadas. _____

4. ¿Quieres las anuales blancas? _____

5. ¿Quieres las etiquetas rosadas? _____

6. ¿Qué quieres? _____

7. Quiero diez y seis flats amarillos. _____

8. Quiero doce plantas verdes. _____

9. ¿Quieres los flats azules? _____

10. ¿Quieres dos macetas moradas? _____

Traduzca al español.

1. I want ten green pots. _____

2. I want five yellow flats. _____

3. Do you want the pink annuals? _____

4. Do you want the purple perennials? _____

5. What do you want? _____

6. I want twenty blue tags. _____

7. I want three orange pots. _____

8. Do you want the black containers? _____

9. Do you want the white hanging baskets? _____

10. What do you want? _____

REPASO

Traduzca al inglés.

1. Envuelve las plantas. _____

2. Consigue las plantas. _____

3. ¿Qué quieres? Carga las paletas. _____

4. Replantar las anuales. _____

5. Saca las hierbas de las canastas colgadas. _____

6. ¿Qué quieres? Pon los precios. _____

7. Consigue el carrito. _____

8. Envuelve los perennes. _____

9. Mueve el recipiente. _____

10. Corta la mala de las plantas. _____

11. ¿Sol o sombra? _____

12. Prepara la mesa de plantar. _____

Traduzca al español.

1. Tag the annuals. _____

2. Move the hanging baskets. _____

3. Dig up the plants. _____

4. Put the plants in the sun. _____

5. Sun or shade? _____

6. What do you want? Get the pot. _____

7. Load the pallet. _____

8. Wrap the perennials. _____

9. What do you want? Tag the prices. _____

10. Repot the plants. _____

11. Deadhead the annuals. _____

12. Put the plants in the shade. _____

Lea el diálogo en voz alta en inglés. Seguidamente tradúzcalo al español.

(in the tennis club)

Sarah: Do you want to play more tennis, Judy?

Judy: No. I'm tired. Do you want to play on Thursday?

Sarah: Yes . . . At what time?

Judy: At ten or ten thirty?

Sarah: At ten. Where are you going?

Judy: I'm going to Tall Trees Nursery. It's spring!

(at Tall Trees Nursery)

Leo: Welcome to Tall Trees, Judy!

Judy: Thank you. I am nervous. It's my first day!

Leo: Do you speak Spanish, Judy?

Judy: Yes. . . a little.

Lea el diálogo en voz alta en español. Seguidamente tradúzcalo al inglés.

(en el club de tennis)

Sarah: ¿Quieres jugar más tenis, Judy?

Judy: No. Estoy cansada. ¿Quieres jugar el jueves?

Sarah: Sí. . . ¿A qué hora?

Judy: ¿A las diez o diez y media?

Sarah: A las diez. ¿A dónde vas?

Judy: Voy a Tall Trees Nursery. ¡Es primavera!

(a Tall Trees Nursery)

Leo: ¡Bienvenidos a Tall Trees, Judy!

Judy: Gracias. Estoy nerviosa. ¡Es mi primer día!

Leo: ¿Hablas español, Judy?

Judy: Sí. . . un poco.

Leo:	Come with me. . .		**Leo:**	Ven conmigo. . .
Judy:	What do you want?		**Judy:**	¿Qué quieres?
Leo:	First deadhead the perennials.		**Leo:**	Primero corta la mala de las perennes.
Judy:	And take out the weeds?		**Judy:**	¿Y saco las hierbas?
Leo:	Yes. Repot the white annuals.		**Leo:**	Sí. Replanta las anuales blancas.
Judy:	In plastic or clay pots?		**Judy:**	¿En macetas de plástico o barro?
Leo:	Clay. Water the hanging baskets.		**Leo:**	De barro. Riega las canastas colgadas.
Judy:	Tag the prices and names?		**Judy:**	¿Pongo los precios y nombres?
Leo:	Yes. You are very organized, Judy.		**Leo:**	Sí. Eres muy organizada, Judy.
Judy:	Thank you.		**Judy:**	Gracias.
Leo:	You're a hard worker!		**Leo:**	¡Eres muy trabajadora!
Customer:	Good morning.		**Cliente:**	Buenos días.
Judy:	Hello. What would you like?		**Judy:**	Hola. . . ¿Qué quieres?
Customer:	I want two flats of red annuals.		**Cliente:**	Quiero dos flats de anuales rojas.
Judy:	What else?		**Judy:**	¿Qué más?
Customer:	Two flats of pink perennials.		**Cliente:**	Dos flats de perennes rosadas.
Judy:	Do you want a cart?		**Judy:**	¿Quieres un carrito?
Customer:	Yes. Perfect!		**Cliente:**	Sí. ¡Perfecto!
Judy:	Do you want a bag of peat moss?		**Judy:**	¿Quieres un saco de turba?
Customer:	Yes and a bag of mulch and fertilizer.		**Cliente:**	Sí y un saco de mezcla y fertilizante.
Judy:	Do you want pine straw or compost?		**Judy:**	¿Quieres paja o abono?
Customer:	No, thank you.		**Cliente:**	No, gracias.
Judy:	Very good. It's forty dollars.		**Judy:**	Muy bien. Es cuarenta dólares.
(Customer attempts to carry it all)			(Cliente trata de llevarlo todo)	
Judy:	Octavio, help the woman, please.		**Judy:**	Octavio, ayuda a la mujer, por favor.
Customer:	Thanks a lot, Octavio. Good bye.		**Cliente:**	Muchas gracias, Octavio. Adios.

Traduzca al español.

1. Welcome! What's your name? _____

2. Nice to meet you. Same to you. _____

3. It's important. It's not correct. _____

4. Everything else is perfect! _____

5. Monday, Wednesday, Friday _____

6. Do you want to play cards? _____

7. Do you want to eat? _____

8. The crew is tired. Are you sick? _____

9. My uncle is the foreman. _____

10. Does your ankle hurt? _____

11. Where is the first aid kit? _____

12. Blow the leaves. Did you plant the shrubs? _____

13. There are five blowers and five rakes. _____

14. Wear the safety glasses and gloves. _____

15. The neighbor is worried and angry. _____

LA CULTURA: CONSEJOS SOBRE EL LIDERAZGO PARA LATINOS

A medida que las empresas anglosajonas van creciendo, buscan empleados latinos para que asuman puestos de mando. Pero lo que los anglosajones no comprenden es que muchos latinos tienden a *acomodarse* en el trabajo que tengan. Muchos latinos sacrificarán la posibilidad de adquirir riqueza porque prefieren la seguridad.

Al trabajar en empresas anglosajonas, los latinos se encuentran ante una encrucijada. Pueden luchar para mantener un trabajo seguro, pero mal pagado, y avanzar *poco a poquito* o pueden reconocer y aprovechar una gran oportunidad. Para ser un líder latino de éxito en los Estados Unidos, además de aprender acerca de las dos culturas, usted necesita:

1. **Estudiar la cultura en este libro y en otros libros.**

2. **Aprender inglés.**

Las buenas empresas dependen de comunicaciones eficaces y por esa razón es importante que los latinos que tienen relaciones con empresas anglosajonas hablan el mismo idioma. La mayoría de los anglosajones hablan inglés únicamente. A pesar de que contratan empleados que hablan español, los anglosajones consideran que no tienen que aprender español. Si un latino quiere tener éxito trabajando en los Estados Unidos, es esencial aprender inglés. Es la habilidad más fundamental en el mundo del trabajo.

3. **Confiar en los demás.**

Ésta es la característica más controversial de los latinos. Antes de confiar en los demás, muchos latinos piensan que primero hay que estudiar a la gente, examinando a cada persona muy detenidamente. Piensan que es mejor asegurarse primero que lamentarlo después. Al principio, esto parece razonable, pero en último término no lo es. La falta de confianza y la cautela excesiva crea más desconfianza y más cautela hasta el punto en que todos desconfían de todos. Si una persona piensa que es honesta y digna de confianza, los demás la verán de ese modo también. La confianza engendra confianza y la desconfianza engendra desconfianza. Ésta es una actitud positiva que vale la pena mantener toda la vida.

4. Cambie su actitud de "No hacerme notar."

Los latinos vacilan a la hora de expresar sus opiniones. Por su parte, a los anglos les cuesta aguantarse y tener que esperar para expresar las suyas. Las opiniones y las ideas son la base para el éxito comercial. Los anglos valoran mucho las opiniones de los latinos; sin embargo, los empleados latinos permanecen silenciosos. Puesto que muchos latinos están trabajando en las actividades fundamentales de las empresas, tienen mucha información en sus manos, por ejemplo, sobre lo que funciona y lo que no funciona en su lugar de trabajo. Los latinos deben creer en sí mismos y dar sus valiosas opiniones. Aprender a ser más francos y abiertos con los sentimientos, opiniones y asuntos íntimos también les ayudará a construir relaciones de confianza que duren largo tiempo.

5. Haga siempre lo que usted dice que hará.

Para tener éxito en los negocios, así como en la vida, recuerde las letras: DWYSYWD. En inglés hacia delante y hacia atrás estas iniciales significan: *Do what you say you will do*, es decir, "Haga lo que usted dice que hará"; o, como se dice en español: *Dicho y hecho:* "Una vez dicho, así se hace." Asegúrese de cumplir todas las promesas que haga. Quizá parezca un estereotipo, pero en gran medida el latino por naturaleza se siente bien si no cumple del todo un compromiso o una promesa. Quizá es la renuencia del latino a decir "no." Si usted no puede hacer lo que prometió que haría o algo sale mal, dígaselo a su jefe o a su cliente tan pronto como usted lo sepa. Le puede pasar a cualquiera. En muchos casos los demás le ayudarán a resolver el problema.

¿Los inmigrantes latinos están condenados a convertirse en una clase inferior aislada de las demás? ¿Serán siempre los "pobres que trabajan?" Los latinos deben comprender este punto de vista y una vez que tomen conciencia de esta situación, podrán cambiarla. Los latinos son el puente entre las diversas regiones de América. Las compañías cometerían un gran error si no contratan y ascienden a los latinos. . . y lo saben.

Las empresas necesitan a los latinos. Se lo están poniendo fácil a los latinos. Ahora, como latino, usted debe reconocer que hay ciertos factores en su conducta que pueden ser obstáculos para su éxito. Una vez que sepa cuáles son esos obstáculos usted podrá superarlos. Tenga fe en sí mismo. Usted tiene mucho que ofrecer. Es un gran momento para ser latinos bilingües y biculturales en los Estados Unidos.

11

Los Sitios Comerciales y Residenciales

PARTE I LOS SITIOS COMERCIALES

el edificio
building

los apartamentos
apartments

el mall
shopping mall

el aparcamiento
parking lot

el banco
bank

la tienda
store

la iglesia
church

el hospital
hospital

el hotel
hotel

el parque
park

el restaurante
restaurant

el cementerio
cemetery

la escuela
school

la universidad
university

la biblioteca
library

EJERCICIO DE CORRESPONDENCIA

Escriba la letra de cada dibujo al lado de la palabra inglesa que corresponda abajo.

a.

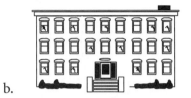
b.

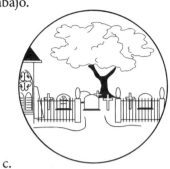
c.

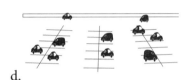
d.

e.

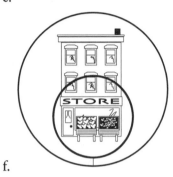
f.

g.

h.

i.

j.

k.

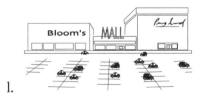
l.

1. _____ school
2. _____ mall
3. _____ cemetery
4. _____ park
5. _____ library
6. _____ apartments

7. _____ building
8. _____ hospital
9. _____ university
10. _____ parking lot
11. _____ church
12. _____ store

EJERCICIO DE VOCABULARIO

Escriba la palabra inglesa abajo.

1. _____ 2. _____ 3. _____

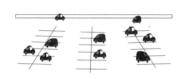

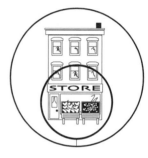

4. _____ 5. _____ 6. _____

8. _____ 9. _____

7. _____

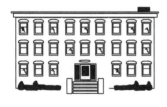

10. _____ 11. _____ 12. _____

EJERCICIO DE CORRESPONDENCIA

Escriba la letra de la palabra en español junto a la palabra inglesa que corresponda a la izquierda.

1. _____ bank
2. _____ church
3. _____ hospital
4. _____ building
5. _____ apartments
6. _____ shopping mall
7. _____ store
8. _____ parking lot

9. _____ hotel
10. _____ park
11. _____ restaurant
12. _____ library
13. _____ cemetery
14. _____ school
15. _____ university

a. la iglesia
b. la biblioteca
c. el cementerio
d. el hotel
e. la escuela
f. el hospital
g. la tienda
h. el restaurante

i. el edificio
j. el parque
k. el banco
l. el aparcamiento
m. los apartamentos
n. la universidad
o. el mall

CRUCIGRAMAS

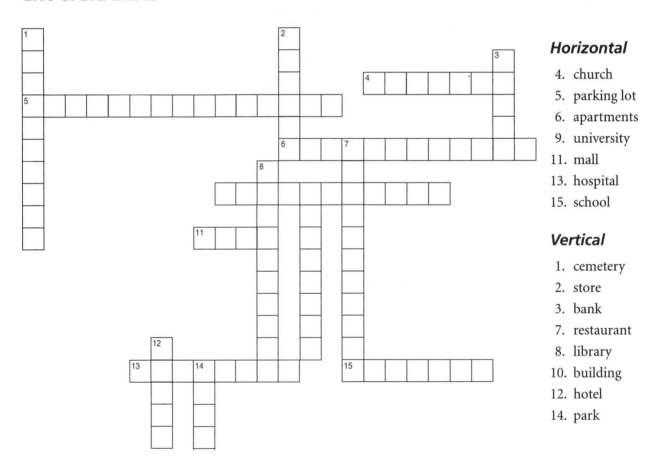

Horizontal

4. church
5. parking lot
6. apartments
9. university
11. mall
13. hospital
15. school

Vertical

1. cemetery
2. store
3. bank
7. restaurant
8. library
10. building
12. hotel
14. park

Horizontal

3. universidad
7. tienda
9. hospital
11. restaurante
12. biblioteca
13. aparcamiento
14. banco
15. escuela

Vertical

1. cementerio
2. edificio
4. mall
5. apartamentos
6. iglesia
8. hotel
10. parque

EJERCICIO DE TRADUCCIÓN

Traduzca al inglés.

1. la tienda _____

2. el edificio _____

3. el parque _____

4. el banco _____

5. el cementerio _____

6. el hotel _____

7. el aparcamiento _____

8. la escuela _____

9. el hospital _____

10. el restaurante _____

11. los apartamentos _____

12. la universidad _____

13. el mall _____

14. la iglesia _____

15. la biblioteca _____

Traduzca al español.

1. park _____

2. restaurant _____

3. cemetery _____

4. church _____

5. university _____

6. school _____

7. bank _____

8. library _____

9. shopping mall _____

10. store _____

11. parking lot _____

12. hotel _____

13. hospital _____

14. building _____

15. apartments _____

OPCIONES MÚLTIPLES

Marque con un círculo la letra de la respuesta correcta.

1. **school**
   a. la escuela
   b. el edificio
   c. el parque
   d. el banco

2. **church**
   a. la universidad
   b. el mall
   c. la iglesia
   d. la biblioteca

3. **park**
   a. el edificio
   b. el parque
   c. el banco
   d. el aparcamiento

4. **restaurant**
   a. el hotel
   b. la escuela
   c. el hospital
   d. el restaurante

5. **cemetery**
   a. el edificio
   b. el parque
   c. el banco
   d. el cementerio

6. **university**
   a. la escuela
   b. el edificio
   c. la universidad
   d. el hospital

7. **building**
   a. el edificio
   b. la escuela
   c. la biblioteca
   d. el aparcamiento

8. **store**
   a. la universidad
   b. la escuela
   c. la tienda
   d. el edificio

9. **bank**
   a. la biblioteca
   b. el banco
   c. la iglesia
   d. la escuela

10. **apartments**
    a. el hotel
    b. el hospital
    c. el aparcamiento
    d. los apartamentos

LA GRAMÁTICA: ¿A DÓNDE VAS?

ir	**to go**
¿A dónde vas?	**Where are you going?**
Voy	**I'm going, I go**
Vamos	**We're going, We go**
Va	**John's going, John goes**

Traduzca al inglés.

1. Voy _____

2. Vamos _____

3. ¿A dónde vas? _____

4. Va _____

5. Voy _____

6. Vamos _____

Traduzca al español.

1. Where are you going? _____

2. I'm going _____

3. Mary is going _____

4. We go _____

5. We're going _____

6. I go _____

LA GRAMÁTICA: "IR" Y LUGARES

Para expresar al, a los, a la, y a las, en inglés, hay solamente una forma: "to the." Estudie los ejemplos siguientes.

Voy **a la** tienda.	I'm going **to the** store.
Voy **a las** oficinas.	I'm going **to the** offices.
Voy **al** banco.	I'm going **to the** bank.
Voy **a los** apartamentos.	I'm going **to the** apartments.

EJERCICIO ORAL

¿A dónde vas? Imagínese que es sábado por la mañana. Trabaje con un compañero preguntando y respondiendo a dónde va a ir cada uno de ustedes durante el fin de semana. Use la pregunta: *Where are you going?* Sigue el modelo.

STUDENT A:	Where are you going?
STUDENT B:	I'm going to. . .

1.   2.   3.   4.

5.   6.   7.   8.

PARTE II LOS SITIOS RESIDENCIALES

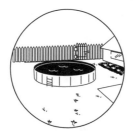

la casa
house

la alberca
pool

el garaje
garage

la banqueta
sidewalk

la calzada
driveway

el jardín de enfrente
front yard

el jardín de atrás
back yard

el estanque
pond

la fuente
fountain

la calle
street

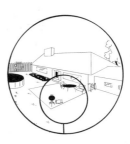

el patio
patio

el perro
dog

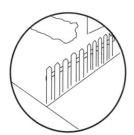

la cerca
fence

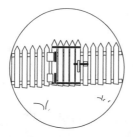

la puerta
gate

el sendero
path

EJERCICIO DE CORRESPONDENCIA

Escriba la letra de cada dibujo a lado de la palabra inglesa que corresponde abajo.

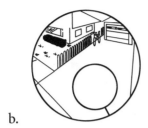 a.

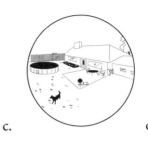 b.

 c.

 d.

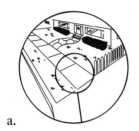 e.

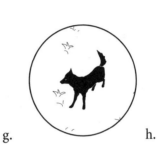 f.

 g.

 h.

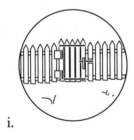 i.

 j.

 k.

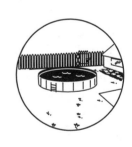 l.

1. _____ pond

2. _____ dog

3. _____ house

4. _____ pool

5. _____ gate

6. _____ sidewalk

7. _____ path

8. _____ back yard

9. _____ street

10. _____ fence

11. _____ front yard

12. _____ driveway

EJERCICIO DE VOCABULARIO

Escriba la palabra inglesa abajo.

1. _____ 2. _____ 3. _____ 4. _____

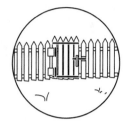 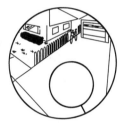  

5. _____ 6. _____ 7. _____ 8. _____

9. _____ 10. _____ 11. _____ 12. _____

EJERCICIO DE CORRESPONDENCIA

Escriba la letra de la palabra en español junto a la palabra inglesa que corresponda a la izquierda.

1. _____ sidewalk
2. _____ driveway
3. _____ front yard
4. _____ house
5. _____ pool
6. _____ garage
7. _____ back yard
8. _____ pond

9. _____ patio
10. _____ dog
11. _____ fence
12. _____ gate
13. _____ path
14. _____ fountain
15. _____ street

a. el jardín de atrás
b. el estanque
c. la fuente
d. el garaje
e. la cerca
f. la casa
g. la puerta
h. la banqueta

i. el sendero
j. el jardín de enfrente
k. la alberca
l. la calzada
m. la calle
n. el patio
o. el perro

CRUCIGRAMAS

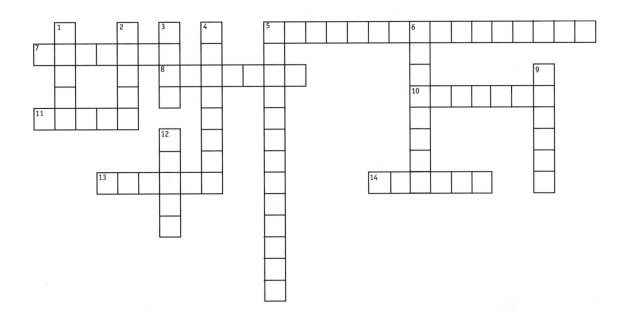

Horizontal

5. front yard
7. driveway
8. path
10. pool
11. dog
13. gate

Vertical

1. street
2. patio
3. house
4. sidewalk
5. back yard
6. pond
9. garage
12. fence
14. fountain

Horizontal

3. perro
4. fuente
6. garaje
8. jardín de atrás
9. estanque
11. sendero
12. banqueta
13. cerca

Vertical

1. casa
2. patio
3. calzada
5. puerta
7. jardín de enfrente
10. alberca
12. calle

EJERCICIO DE TRADUCCIÓN

Traduzca al inglés.

1. el jardín de atrás _____
2. el estanque _____
3. la fuente _____
4. el perro _____
5. la calzada _____
6. el jardín de enfrente _____
7. la calle _____
8. la cerca _____
9. la puerta _____
10. el patio _____
11. el sendero _____
12. la casa _____
13. la alberca _____
14. el garaje _____
15. la banqueta _____

Traduzca al español.

1. pool _____
2. garage _____
3. sidewalk _____
4. driveway _____
5. house _____
6. back yard _____
7. gate _____
8. path _____
9. pond _____
10. patio _____
11. fountain _____
12. street _____
13. front yard _____
14. dog _____
15. fence _____

OPCIONES MÚLTIPLES

Marque con un círculo la letra de la respuesta correcta.

1. **driveway**
   a. la calzada
   b. la calle
   c. la cerca
   d. la casa

2. **dog**
   a. la puerta
   b. el perro
   c. el patio
   d. la cerca

3. **house**
   a. la calzada
   b. la calle
   c. la cerca
   d. la casa

4. **back yard**
   a. la frente
   b. el jardín de enfrente
   c. el jardín de atrás
   d. la banqueta

5. **gate**
   a. la puerta
   b. la cerca
   c. la alberca
   d. la fuente

6. **path**
   a. la banqueta
   b. el sendero
   c. la estanque
   d. la calzada

7. **pond**
   a. el garaje
   b. la alberca
   c. la cerca
   d. la estanque

8. **pool**
   a. la puerta
   b. la cerca
   c. la alberca
   d. la fuente

9. **fence**
   a. la puerta
   b. la cerca
   c. la alberca
   d. la fuente

10. **sidewalk**
    a. la banqueta
    b. el sendero
    c. la alberca
    d. la calzada

11. **street**
    a. la calzada
    b. la calle
    c. la cerca
    d. la casa

12. **front yard**
    a. el jardín de enfrente
    b. la fuente
    c. el sendero
    d. el jardín de atrás

LA GRAMÁTICA: "IR" EN EL PASADO

Usted aprendió recientemente a expresar dónde va una persona usando el verbo "*to go.*" Para hablar acerca de adonde fue una persona, usted usa el pasado de esta misma palabra.

¿A dónde fuiste?	**Where did you go?**
Fui	**I went**
Fue	**Joe went**
Fuimos	**We went**

Traduzca al inglés.

1. Fuí _____

2. Fuimos _____

3. ¿A dónde fuiste? _____

4. Fue _____

5. Fuí _____

6. Fuimos _____

Traduzca al español.

1. Where did you go? _____

2. I went _____

3. Mary went _____

4. We went _____

5. I went _____

6. Where did you go? _____

EJERCICIO ORAL

¿A dónde fuiste? Imagínese que es un viernes por la tarde. Trabaje con un compañero preguntando y respondiendo adonde fueron en el sitio de trabajo. Use: *Where did you go?* Sigue el modelo.

STUDENT A:	Where did you go?
STUDENT B:	I went to. . .

1.

2.

3.

4.

5.

6.

7.

8.

REPASO

Traduzca al inglés.

1. ¿A dónde vas? _____
2. Voy al jardín de atrás. _____
3. Vamos a la iglesia. _____
4. Juan va a la tienda. _____
5. Voy a la escuela. _____
6. ¿A dónde fuiste? _____
7. Fui a la calzada. _____
8. Teresa fue al garaje. _____
9. Fuimos al edificio. _____
10. Ana fue a la alberca. _____

Traduzca al español.

1. Where are you going? _____
2. I'm going to the store. _____
3. He's going to the bank. _____
4. We're going to the parking lot. _____
5. Where did you go? _____
6. I went to the parking lot. _____
7. We went to the back yard. _____
8. Thomas went to the bank. _____
9. We went to the house. _____
10. I went to the building. _____

Traduzca al español.

1. Welcome! What's your name? _____
2. Nice to meet you. Same to you. _____
3. It's important. It's not correct. _____
4. Everything else is perfect! _____
5. Monday, Wednesday, Friday _____
6. Do you want to play cards? _____
7. Do you want to eat? _____
8. The crew is tired. Are you sick? _____
9. My uncle is the foreman. _____
10. Does your ankle hurt? _____
11. Where is the first aid kit? _____
12. Blow the leaves. Did you plant the shrubs? _____
13. There are five blowers and five rakes. _____
14. Wear the safety glasses and gloves. _____
15. The neighbor is worried and angry. _____

Lea el diálogo en voz alta en inglés.
Seguidamente tradúzcalo al español.

(driving in the truck)

Kevin: Welcome to Chicago!

Guillermo: Thanks, Kevin.

Kevin: Do you like to listen to music?

Guillermo: Yes, a lot. I like salsa music.

Kevin: Help me.

Guillermo: (moves the dial) What time is it?

Kevin: It's ten o'clock.

Guillermo: Fantastic! (then finds the radio station)

Kevin: Okay. I like the music.

Guillermo: Where are you going?

Kevin: First . . . to the Catholic church.

Guillermo: Are there masses (*misas*)?

Kevin: Yes . . . on Sundays.

Guillermo: At what time?

Kevin: At eight, ten, and twelve o'clock.

Guillermo: Do you go to church, Kevin?

Kevin: Yes, I go with my wife and my children.

Guillermo: Where is the bank?

Kevin: (points) The red brick building.

Guillermo: Very good! I like the pond.

Kevin: Thank you. Do you like the yellow flowers?

Guillermo: Yes, a lot! Where are we going?

Kevin: We're going to the hospital and the apartments.

(an hour later at Kevin's house)

Kevin: Where is your mother, Beth?

Beth: She went to the store.

Kevin: Beth, I'd like to introduce you to Guillermo.

Beth: Nice to meet you.

Kevin: No . . . remember, Beth? . . . "*Mucho gusto.*"

Beth: Oh, yeah. ¡*Mucho gusto!*

Guillermo: Same to you!

Beth: Where are you from, Guillermo?

Lea el diálogo en voz alta en español.
Seguidamente tradúzcalo al inglés.

(viajando por camión)

Kevin: ¡Bienvenidos a Chicago!

Guillermo: Gracias, Kevin.

Kevin: ¿Te gusta escuchar la música?

Guillermo: Sí, mucho. Me gusta la música salsa.

Kevin: Ayúdame.

Guillermo: (sintoniza al radio) ¿Qué hora es?

Kevin: Son las diez.

Guillermo: ¡Fántastico! (encuentra la estación del radio)

Kevin: Está bien. Me gusta la música.

Guillermo: ¿A dónde vas?

Kevin: Primero . . . a la iglesia católica.

Guillermo: ¿Hay misas (*masses*)?

Kevin: Sí . . . los domingos.

Guillermo: ¿A qué hora?

Kevin: A las ocho, diez y doce.

Guillermo: ¿Vas a la iglesia, Kevin?

Kevin: Sí, voy con mi esposa y mis hijos.

Guillermo: ¿Dónde está el banco?

Kevin: (señala) El edificio con ladrillo rojo.

Guillermo: ¡Muy bien! Me gusta el estanque.

Kevin: Gracias. ¿Te gustan las flores amarillas?

Guillermo: ¡Sí, mucho! ¿A dónde vamos?

Kevin: Vamos al hospital y los apartamentos.

(una hora más tarde en la casa de Kevin)

Kevin: ¿Dónde está tu mamá, Beth?

Beth: Fue a la tienda.

Kevin: Beth, quiero presentarte a Guillermo.

Beth: Nice to meet you.

Kevin: No . . . ¿recuerdas, Beth? . . . "*Mucho gusto.*"

Beth: Ah, si. ¡*Mucho gusto!*

Guillermo: ¡Igualmente!

Beth: ¿De dónde eres, Guillermo?

Traduzca al español.

1. I'm studying Spanish. _____

2. Do you speak English? _____

3. Come with me. _____

4. You're a hard worker! _____

5. The crew is in a bad mood. _____

6. The manager is busy. _____

7. Get the blower. _____

8. Mix the oil and the gas. _____

9. Use the pick and the sledge hammer. _____

10. Be careful! Pay attention! Drive slowly! _____

11. Does your ankle hurt? Your back? _____

12. Miguel blows the leaves. _____

13. The crew prunes the shrubs. _____

14. My brother spreads out the mulch. _____

15. The crew leader applies the fertilizer. _____

LA CULTURA: NOMBRES Y APODOS

La importancia de la familia en la cultura latina se aprecia en el sistema español de apellidos. La mayoría de los latinos tienen dos apellidos. Este sistema confunde a muchos empleados que trabajan en las oficinas de personal de las organizaciones estadounidenses.

El apellido del padre aparece primero seguido por el apellido de la madre. Juan Martínez López tiene un padre de apellido Martínez y una madre cuyo apellido de soltera es López. Si Ana, la hermana de Juan, se casa con Javier Hernández Rodríguez, ella conserva el apellido del padre, pierde el apellido de su madre y se convierte en Ana Martínez de Hernández.

Los apodos son populares en ambas culturas. En inglés, el apodo para Robert es Bob, para William es Bill y para Michael es Mike. En español, los apodos comunes son Pepe para José, Paco para Francisco y Memo para Guillermo. En inglés, los niños a menudo usan la forma diminutiva de su nombre. En inglés el nombre en diminutivo termina en -y o en -ie y en español los nombres terminan en -ito o -ita.

Muchos apelativos de cariño en la cultura latina pueden sorprender a los anglos. Gordo, flaco y pelón se usan en muchas ocasiones con cariño y sin intención de ofender a la persona. En los Estados Unidos ocurre lo contrario. Este tipo de sobrenombres se utiliza a menudo por crueldad.

El nombre de una persona es importante para ella. Es esencial aprender a pronunciar bien y escribir correctamente los nombres de sus compañeros de trabajo.

12

Las Direcciones y Los Lugares

PARTE I   LAS DIRECCIONES

norte	**north**
sur	**south**
este	**east**
oeste	**west**
derecha	**right**
izquierda	**left**
derecho	**straight ahead**
solamente	**only**
aquí	**here**
por aquí	**around here**
allí	**there**
allá	**over there**
lejos	**far**
cerca	**near**

EJERCICIO DE CORRESPONDENCIA

Escriba la letra de la palabra en español junto a la palabra inglesa que corresponda a la izquierda.

1. _____ south	8. _____ east	a. derecha	h. oeste
2. _____ there	9. _____ around here	b. lejos	i. allí
3. _____ near	10. _____ left	c. aquí	j. norte
4. _____ right	11. _____ over there	d. sur	k. solamente
5. _____ here	12. _____ far	e. cerca	l. este
6. _____ west	13. _____ straight ahead	f. derecho	m. izquierda
7. _____ only	14. _____ north	g. allá	n. por aquí

CRUCIGRAMAS

Horizontal

1. far
4. right
5. around here
7. south
8. only
11. left
12. near

Vertical

2. west
3. over there
4. straight ahead
6. east
9. here
10. north
13. there

Horizontal

1. cerca
3. allá
5. aquí
8. sur
10. oeste
11. derecho
13. solamente

Vertical

1. norte
2. derecha
4. allí
6. este
7. izquierda
9. lejos
12. por aquí

EJERCICIO DE TRADUCCIÓN

Traduzca al inglés.

1. norte _____
2. sur _____
3. lejos _____
4. cerca _____
5. derecha _____
6. izquierda _____
7. derecho _____
8. este _____
9. oeste _____
10. aquí _____
11. allí _____
12. por aquí _____
13. allá _____
14. solamente _____

Traduzca al español.

1. near _____
2. far _____
3. north _____
4. south _____
5. here _____
6. around here _____
7. there _____
8. over there _____
9. straight ahead _____
10. left _____
11. right _____
12. east _____
13. west _____
14. only _____

OPCIONES MÚLTIPLES

Marque con un círculo la letra de la respuesta correcta.

1. **near**
   a. norte
   b. sur
   c. lejos
   d. cerca

2. **right**
   a. derecha
   b. izquierda
   c. derecho
   d. este

3. **here**
   a. allá
   b. aquí
   c. allí
   d. por aquí

4. **only**
   a. solamente
   b. oeste

   c. derecho
   d. este

5. **far**
   a. norte
   b. sur
   c. lejos
   d. cerca

6. **left**
   a. derecha
   b. izquierda
   c. derecho
   d. lejos

7. **over there**
   a. aquí
   b. allí
   c. por aquí
   d. allá

8. **around here**
   a. este
   b. oeste
   c. por aquí
   d. por allí

9. **west**
   a. este
   b. oeste
   c. aquí
   d. allí

10. **only**
    a. oeste
    b. aquí
    c. solamente
    d. allá

PARTE II   LOS LUGARES

en
in, on

encima
on top

arriba
up, above

abajo
down, below

delante
in front

detrás
behind

entre
between

alrededor
around

dentro
inside

fuera
outside

sobre
over

EJERCICIO DE CORRESPONDENCIA

Escriba la letra de cada dibujo al lado de la palabra inglesa que corresponda abajo.

a.

b.

c.

d.

e.

f.

g.

h.

i.

1. _____ on top

2. _____ up, above

3. _____ in front

4. _____ around

5. _____ below

6. _____ inside

7. _____ between

8. _____ behind

9. _____ outside

EJERCICIO DE VOCABULARIO

Escriba la palabra inglesa abajo.

1. _____

2. _____

3. _____

4. _____

5. _____

6. _____

7. _____

8. _____

9. _____

EJERCICIO DE CORRESPONDENCIA

Escriba la letra de la palabra en español junto a la palabra inglesa que corresponda a la izquierda.

1. _____ between
2. _____ over
3. _____ on top
4. _____ up, above
5. _____ in front

6. _____ outside
7. _____ down, below
8. _____ around
9. _____ inside
10. _____ behind

a. abajo
b. alrededor
c. dentro
d. detrás
e. entre

f. sobre
g. encima
h. arriba
i. delante
j. fuera

CRUCIGRAMAS

Horizontal

2. down, below
5. in, on
6. behind
8. around
10. on top

Vertical

1. outside
2. up, above
3. inside
4. between
7. over
9. in front

Horizontal	**Vertical**
2. sobre	1. detrás
5. entre	2. fuera
6. encima	3. delante
7. dentro	4. alrededor

EJERCICIO DE TRADUCCIÓN

Traduzca al inglés.

1. dentro _____
2. arriba _____
3. sobre _____
4. fuera _____
5. alrededor _____
6. detrás _____
7. delante _____
8. entre _____
9. abajo _____
10. encima _____

Traduzca al español.

1. between _____
2. over _____
3. on top _____
4. up, above _____
5. in front _____
6. outside _____
7. down, below _____
8. around _____
9. inside _____
10. behind _____

OPCIONES MÚLTIPLES

Marque con un círculo la letra de la respuesta correcta.

1. **outside**
   a. dentro
   b. arriba
   c. sobre
   d. fuera

2. **in front**
   a. alrededor
   b. detrás
   c. delante
   d. entre

3. **down, below**
   a. abajo
   b. encima
   c. detrás
   d. delante

4. **up, above**
   a. dentro
   b. alrededor

   c. sobre
   d. arriba

5. **behind**
   a. detrás
   b. delante
   c. fuera
   d. entre

6. **around**
   a. abajo
   b. en
   c. alrededor
   d. encima

7. **in, on**
   a. encima
   b. en
   c. entre
   d. abajo

8. **between**
   a. entre
   b. en
   c. encima
   d. sobre

9. **outside**
   a. dentro
   b. delante
   c. fuera
   d. arriba

10. **over**
    a. arriba
    b. sobre
    c. delante
    d. detrás

EJERCICIO ORAL

¡Cuidado con el perro! Muchos lugares residenciales tienen perros. Imagínese que usted tiene miedo de ellos. Trabaje con un compañero. Pregunte y responda: *Where is the dog?* (¿Dónde está el perro?) Sigue el modelo.

STUDENT A: Where is the dog?
STUDENT B: The dog is in the house.

1.

2.

3.

4.

5.

6.

REPASO

Traduzca al español.

1. Where is the doghouse? _____

2. The doghouse is not far, it's close. _____

3. The doghouse is over there. _____

4. Where? Straight ahead? _____

5. On the left? No, on the right. _____

6. Where is the dog? _____

7. The dog is inside the doghouse. _____

8. No, the dog is behind the doghouse. _____

9. The dog is outside? _____

10. Yes, the dog is here! _____

Lea el diálogo en voz alta en inglés. Seguidamente tradúzcalo al español.

(at the coffee pot)

Randy: Hello. Good morning, Juanito.

Juanito: Hello, boss. How are you?

Randy: Excellent! I'm in a good mood!

Juanito: Why?

Randy: Because it's my birthday!

Juanito: The twenty ninth of February? There are only twenty eight days in February. . .

Randy: No. It's Leap Year! I'm only seven years old!

(in the parking lot)

Randy: Please, go to Tall Trees Nursery.

Juanito: What do you want?

Randy: I need a bag of soil, peat moss, mulch, and fertilizer.

Juanito: Do you need stones, bricks, and cement?

Randy: Yes.

Juanito: That's a lot! Come with me. Please!

Randy: No. . . no. . . I'm very busy.

Lea el diálogo en voz alta en español. Seguidamente tradúzcalo al inglés.

(alrededor de la cafetera)

Randy: Hola. Buenos días, Juanito.

Juanito: Hola, jefe. ¿Cómo estás?

Randy: ¡Excelente! ¡Estoy de buen humor!

Juanito: ¿Por qué?

Randy: ¡Porque hoy es mi cumpleaños!

Juanito: ¿El veinte y nueve de febrero? Hay solamente veinte y ocho días en febrero. . .

Randy: No. ¡Es el año bisiesto! ¡Tengo solamente siete años!

(en el parque de aparcamiento)

Randy: Por favor, vete a Tall Trees Nursery.

Juanito: ¿Qué quieres?

Randy: Necesito un saco de tierra, turba, mezcla y fertilizante.

Juanito: ¿Necesitas piedras, ladrillos y cemento?

Randy: Sí.

Juanito: Es mucho. Ven conmigo. ¡Por favor!

Randy: No. . . no. . . estoy muy ocupado.

Juanito: Where are you going?

Randy: I'm going to the office.

(an hour later)

Randy: Thanks, Juanito. You're a hard worker!

Juanito: And very responsible!

Randy: Yes. . . that's why you're the foreman.

Juanito: I'm the foreman because I speak English, right?

Randy: Yes. Juanito. . . I study Spanish.

Juanito: How do you say *"You're smart for a seven-year-old!"* in Spanish?

Randy: *Eres inteligente para siete años!* How do you say *"Let's go!"* in Spanish?

Juanito: *¡Vamos!*

Randy: Let's go to the mall first.

Juanito: Where is it?

Randy: It's around here.

Juanito: Oh. . . yes. . . near the McDonald's.

Randy: Do you want to eat?

Juanito: Yes. . .

Drive thru: Hello! Good afternoon! What would you like?

Randy: I want four hamburgers and two Cokes.

Drive thru: Six dollars, please.

Randy: Thank you.

Juanito: Randy, here is three dollars.

Randy: No. . . no. . . buy me a beer for my birthday!

Juanito: Is there a party?

Randy: Yes. . . at my house. Around the pool! And in the pool. We're going to play volleyball in the water!

Randy: Do you like to swim?

Juanito: I like to a lot! Where is your house?

Randy: My house is between Oak and Maple Streets.

Juanito: Behind the church and the parking lot?

Juanito: ¿Adónde vas?

Randy: Voy a la oficina.

(una hora más tarde)

Randy: Gracias, Juanito. Eres muy trabajador!

Juanito: ¡Y muy responsable!

Randy: Sí. . . por eso eres el mayordomo.

Juanito: Soy mayordomo porque hablo inglés, ¿no?

Randy: Sí. Juanito. . . estudio español.

Juanito: ¿Como se dice *"You're smart for a seven-year-old!"* en español?

Randy: ¡Eres inteligente para siete años! ¿Cómo se dice *"Let's go!"* en español?

Juanito: ¡Vamos!

Randy: Vamos al mall, primero.

Juanito: ¿Dónde está?

Randy: Está por aquí.

Juanito: Oh. . . sí. . . cerca de McDonald's.

Randy: ¿Quieres comer?

Juanito: Sí. . .

Drive thru: Hola! ¡Buenas tardes! ¿Qué quieres?

Randy: Quiero cuatro hamburguesas y dos Cocas.

Drive thru: Séis dólares, por favor.

Randy: Gracias.

Juanito: Randy, aquí lo tiene tres dólares.

Randy: No. . .no. . . cómprame una cerveza para mi cumpleaños!

Juanito: ¿Hay una fiesta?

Randy: Sí. . . en mi casa. ¡Alrededor de la alberca! Y en la alberca. ¡Vamos a jugar volibol en el agua!

Randy: ¿Te gusta nadar?

Juanito: ¡Me gusta mucho! ¿Dónde está tu casa?

Randy: Mi casa está entre las calles Oak y Maple.

Juanito: ¿Detrás de la iglesia y el aparcamiento?

Randy: Yes. The party is on Friday at 8:00.

(Friday)

Randy: Please . . . prune the shrubs, blow the leaves, and water the flowers.

Juanito: And sweep the sidewalk? With the broom or the push broom?

Randy: I don't care. I'm nervous!

Juanito: Where are you going?

Randy: I'm going to the store. I need pizza, salad, Coke, and beer.

Juanito: And ice *!

*ice – el hielo

Randy: Sí. La fiesta es el viernes a las ocho.

(viernes)

Randy: Por favor. . . poda los arbustos, sopla las hojas, y riega las flores.

Juanito: ¿Y barro la banqueta? ¿Con la escoba o el cepillo?

Randy: No me importa. ¡Estoy nervioso!

Juanito: ¿A dónde vas?

Randy: Voy a la tienda. Necesito pizza, ensalada, Coca y cerveza.

Juanito: ¡Y hielo!

*hielo – ice

Traduzca al español.

1. How's it going? _____
2. Do you speak English? _____
3. Everything else is perfect! _____
4. When? Who? With whom? How many? _____
5. First go to the store and the bank. _____
6. Second go to the parking lots. _____
7. Monday, Friday, Saturday, Sunday _____
8. What's your wife's name? _____
9. The woman is patient. The man is impatient. _____
10. I play billiards on Fridays. Do you like to play? _____
11. My shoulder hurts. Does your neck hurt? _____
12. Drive slowly. Don't touch the blades. _____
13. Wash and put away the shovels and the pruners. _____
14. Plant, water, and mulch the trees. _____
15. Blow and rake the leaves. _____
16. Spread and tamp the soil. Add the mulch. _____
17. Get the stones and the rock. _____
18. Tag the names. Tag the prices. _____
19. Repot the yellow annuals in plastic pots. _____
20. Deadhead the plants. _____

LA CULTURA: DÍAS DE INDEPENDENCIA

País	*Día de Independencia*	*País*	*Día de Independencia*
Argentina	9 de julio	**Honduras**	15 de septiembre
Bolivia	6 de agosto	**México**	16 de septiembre
Chile	18 de septiembre	**Nicaragua**	15 de septiembre
Colombia	20 de julio	**Panama**	28 de noviembre
Costa Rica	15 de septiembre		3 de noviembre
Cuba	20 de mayo	**Paraguay**	14 de mayo
República Dominicana	22 de febrero	**Peru**	28 de julio
Ecuador	3 de octubre	**Estados Unidos**	4 de julio
El Salvador	15 de septiembre	**Uruguay**	25 de agosto
Guatemala	15 de septiembre	**Venezuela**	5 de julio

Días de Fiesta en los Estados Unidos

Valentine's Day	14 de febrero
April Fool's Day	1 de abril
Memorial Day	mayo (ultimo lunes)
Fourth of July	4 de julio
Labor Day	septiembre (primer lunes)
Halloween	31 de octubre
Thanksgiving Day	noviembre (tercer jueves)
Christmas	25 de diciembre
New Year's Eve	31 de diciembre

13

El Agua, Rociar y Regar

PARTE I   EL AGUA, ROCIAR Y REGAR

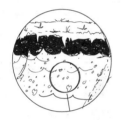

el agua
water

la tierra
soil

la manguera
hose

la zanja
trench

la pipa
pipe

el codo
elbow

la fuga, el escape
leak

la boquilla
nozzle

la válvula
valve

las cabezas
sprinkler heads

el alambre
wire

el rociador
sprinkler

EJERCICIO DE CORRESPONDENCIA

Escriba la letra de cada dibujo al lado de la palabra inglesa que corresponda abajo.

a.

b.

c.

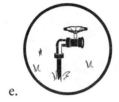

d.

e.

f.

g.

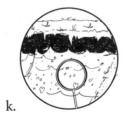

h.

i.

j.

k.

l.

1. _____ elbow

2. _____ sprinkler heads

3. _____ hose

4. _____ wire

5. _____ water

6. _____ trench

7. _____ leak

8. _____ sprinkler

9. _____ soil

10. _____ nozzle

11. _____ pipe

12. _____ valve

EJERCICIO DE VOCABULARIO

Escriba la palabra inglesa abajo.

1. _____

2. _____

3. _____

4. _____

5. _____

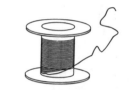

6. _____

7. _____

8. _____

9. _____

10. _____

11. _____

12. _____

EJERCICIO DE CORRESPONDENCIA

Escriba la letra de la palabra en español junto a la palabra inglesa que corresponda a la izquierda.

1. _____ leak
2. _____ nozzle
3. _____ hose
4. _____ wire
5. _____ pipe
6. _____ elbow

7. _____ water
8. _____ soil
9. _____ valve
10. _____ sprinkler heads
11. _____ trench
12. _____ sprinkler

a. el codo
b. la válvula
c. el alambre
d. la zanja
e. la pipa
f. el agua

g. la fuga
h. la boquilla
i. la tierra
j. las cabezas
k. la manguera
l. el rociador

CRUCIGRAMAS

Horizontal

2. water
5. hose
6. soil
8. pipe
9. elbow
10. sprinkler heads
11. nozzle

Vertical

1. valve
2. wire
3. leak
4. trench
7. sprinkler

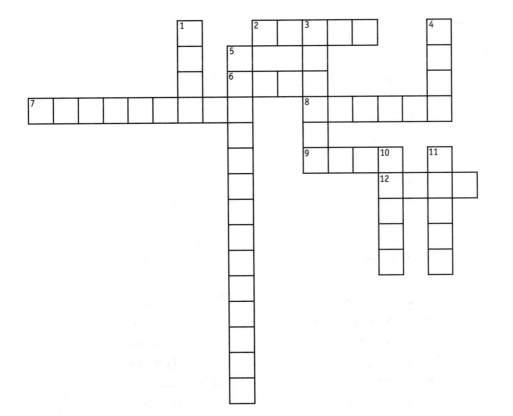

Horizontal

2. agua
6. pipa
7. rociador
8. boquilla
9. manguera
12. fuga

Vertical

1. tierra
3. zanja
4. cable, alambre
5. cabezas
10. codo
11. válvula

EJERCICIO DE TRADUCCIÓN

Traduzca al inglés.

1. la fuga _____
2. las cabezas _____
3. la zanja _____
4. el alambre _____
5. la válvula _____
6. la fuga _____
7. la pipa _____
8. el rociador _____
9. la boquilla _____
10. la manguera _____

Traduzca al español.

1. leak _____
2. sprinkler _____
3. wire _____
4. pipe _____
5. water _____
6. nozzle _____
7. valve _____
8. trench _____
9. elbow _____
10. sprinkler heads _____

OPCIONES MÚLTIPLES

Marque con un círculo la letra de la respuesta correcta.

1. **leak**
   a. la zanja
   b. la tierra
   c. el codo
   d. la fuga, el escape

2. **soil**
   a. la boquilla
   b. la manguera
   c. la tierra
   d. la zanja

3. **water**
   a. la pipa
   b. el rociador
   c. el agua
   d. la manguera

4. **hose**
   a. la manguera
   b. el rociador
   c. el agua
   d. la boquilla

5. **trench**
   a. la boquilla
   b. la manguera
   c. la tierra
   d. la zanja

6. **elbow**
   a. la pipa
   b. el codo
   c. la fuga
   d. la tierra

7. **pipe**
   a. el alambre
   b. la válvula
   c. la zanja
   d. la pipa

8. **nozzle**
   a. la boquilla
   b. la manguera
   c. la tierra
   d. la zanja

9. **valve**
   a. la zanja
   b. la tierra
   c. el codo
   d. la válvula

10. **wire**
    a. el alambre
    b. la válvula
    c. la zanja
    d. la manguera

11. **sprinkler heads**
    a. el agua
    b. el rociador
    c. las cabezas
    d. el alambre

12. **sprinkler**
    a. el agua
    b. el rociador
    c. las cabezas
    d. el alambre

PARTE II TÉRMINOS DE ACCIÓN

Grupo 1		*Grupo 2*	
excava	**dig**	consigue	**get**
corta	**cut**	ajusta	**adjust**
agarra	**hold**	conecta	**connect**
instala	**install**	empuja	**push**
abre	**open**	empaca	**pack**
empareja	**smooth out**	cierra	**close**

Otras palabras de regar	
checa	**check**
saca el agua	**flush**
jala	**pull**
pon	**put**
reemplaza	**replace**

GRUPO 1

Ejercicio de Correspondencia

Escriba la letra de la palabra en español junto a la palabra inglesa que corresponda a la izquierda.

1. _____ install	a. abre
2. _____ dig	b. agarra
3. _____ hold	c. corta
4. _____ smooth out	d. instala
5. _____ open	e. excava
6. _____ cut	f. empareja

Traduzca al inglés.

1. instala _____

2. abre _____

3. corta _____

4. agarra _____

5. empareja _____

6. excava _____

Traduzca al español.

1. open _____

2. smooth out _____

3. dig _____

4. install _____

5. hold _____

6. cut _____

GRUPO 2

Ejercicio de Correspondencia

Escriba la letra de la palabra en español junto a la palabra inglesa que corresponda a la izquierda.

1. _____ adjust   a. empuja
2. _____ close   b. consigue
3. _____ push   c. empaca
4. _____ get   d. conecta
5. _____ pack   e. cierra
6. _____ connect   f. ajusta

Traduzca al inglés.

1. consigue _____
2. ajusta _____
3. empaca _____
4. cierra _____
5. conecta _____
6. empuja _____

Traduzca al español.

1. pack _____
2. connect _____
3. close _____
4. adjust _____
5. get _____
6. push _____

CRUCIGRAMAS

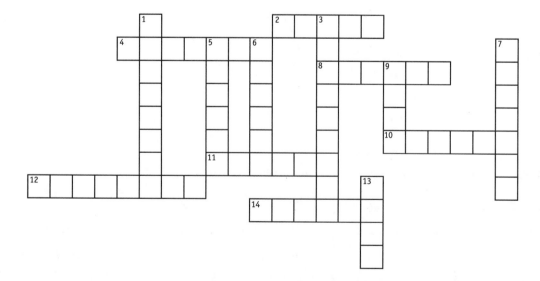

Horizontal

2. cut
4. connect
8. dig
10. push
11. hold
12. smooth out
14. pack

Vertical

1. get
3. replace
5. close
6. adjust
7. install
9. open
13. pull

Horizontal

1. empaca
3. corta
5. excava
7. abre
8. reemplaza
9. empuja
10. instala
12. agarra

Vertical

2. cierra
3. conecta
4. ajusta
6. consigue
9. jala
11. empareja

OPCIONES MÚLTIPLES

Marque con un círculo la letra de la respuesta correcta.

1. dig
   a. corta
   b. consigue
   c. excava
   d. empaca

2. install
   a. ajusta
   b. instala
   c. cierra
   d. abre

3. hold
   a. agarra
   b. ajusta
   c. instala
   d. cierra

4. open
   a. ajusta
   b. instala
   c. cierra
   d. abre

5. cut
   a. conecta
   b. corta
   c. cierra
   d. consigue

6. smooth out
   a. empareja
   b. empaca
   c. empuja
   d. agarra

7. adjust
   a. instala
   b. corta
   c. excava
   d. ajusta

8. get
   a. conecta
   b. corta
   c. cierra
   d. consigue

9. push
   a. empareja
   b. empaca
   c. empuja
   d. agarra

10. connect
   a. conecta
   b. corta
   c. cierra
   d. consigue

11. close
   a. empaca
   b. abre
   c. agarra
   d. cierra

12. pack
   a. excava
   b. empareja
   c. empuja
   d. empaca

LA GRAMÁTICA: ¿PUEDES. . .? CAN YOU. . .?

Para preguntar si alguien puede hacer algo, use las palabras "Can you. . .?"

¿Puedes?	**Can you?**
¿Puedes trabajar el sábado?	**Can you work on Saturday?**
¿Puedes adjustar la válvula?	**Can you adjust the valve?**
¿Puedes conectar la pipa?	**Can you connect the pipe?**
Sí, puedo.	**Yes, I can.**
No, no puedo.	**No, I cannot. (No, I can't.)**

EJERCICIO ORAL

¡La estación del ajetreo! Imagínese que es primavera y que todo el mundo quiere tenerlo todo ahora mismo! Pregúntele a su compañero de trabajo si él puede trabajar algunos días extra este mes. Use: *Can you. . .?* Sigue el modelo.

STUDENT A:	Can you work on Tuesday?
STUDENT B:	Yes, I can.
	No, I cannot. (No, I can't.)

Sunday domingo	Monday lunes	Tuesday martes	Wednesday miércoles	Thursday jueves	Friday viernes	Saturday sábado
	1	2	3	4	5	6
7	8	9	10	11	12	13
14	15	16	17	18	19	20
21	22	23	24	25	26	27
28	29	30	31			

domingo	**Sunday**
lunes	**Monday**
martes	**Tuesday**
miércoles	**Wednesday**
jueves	**Thursday**
viernes	**Friday**
sábado	**Saturday**

REPASO

Traduzca al inglés.

1. Corta la pipa. _____

2. Excava la zanja. _____

3. Abre el agua. _____

4. Empaca la tierra. _____

5. Pon las boquillas. _____

6. Ajusta las cabezas. _____

7. Empareja la tierra. _____

8. Empuja la pipa. _____

9. ¿Puedes conectar la pipa? _____

10. ¿Puedes instalar las cabezas? _____

Traduzca al español.

1. Check the soil. _____

2. Dig a trench. _____

3. Close the valve. _____

4. Install the pipe. _____

5. Adjust the valves. _____

6. Push the pipe. _____

7. Connect the heads. _____

8. Pack the soil. _____

9. Adjust the heads. Can you adjust the heads? _____

10. Cut the pipe. Can you cut the pipe? _____

Lea el diálogo en voz alta en inglés. Seguidamente tradúzcalo al español.

(Monday, July 7)

Chris: Can you work on Saturday, Juan?

Juan: Why? Are you busy?

Chris: Yes.

Juan: At what time?

Chris: At six thirty. . . Is that possible?

Juan: Yes. At six thirty on July 12th.

Chris: That's correct. Can you work on Sunday?

Juan: No, Chris. On Sundays I go to church with my wife and my children.

(Saturday, July 12)

Chris: Be careful and pay attention.

Juan: Are there many cables and wires?

Chris: Yes. Many. . . red, blue, green, yellow . . .

Juan: How do you say the colors in Spanish?

Lea el diálogo en voz alta en español. Seguidamente tradúzcalo al inglés.

(lunes, el 7 de julio)

Chris: ¿Puedes trabajar el sábado, Juan?

Juan: ¿Por qué? ¿Estás muy ocupado?

Chris: Sí.

Juan: ¿A qué hora?

Chris: A las seis y media. . . ¿Es posible?

Juan: Sí. A las seis y media el 12 de julio.

Chris: Es correcto. ¿Puedes trabajar el domingo?

Juan: No, Chris. Los domingos voy a la iglesia con mi esposa y mis hijos.

(sábado, el 12 de julio)

Chris: Ten cuidado y presta atención.

Juan: ¿Hay muchos cables y alambre?

Chris: Sí. Muchos. . .*red, blue, green, yellow.* . .

Juan: ¿Cómo se dice los colores en español?

Chris: Hmmm. . . I'm studying Spanish. . . *rojo, azul, verde, negro, gris, blanco, café, amarillo, rosado, morado y. . . ana. . . anaran. . .*

Juan: Do it like me! A- na -ran- ja- do.

Chris: A-na-ran-ja-do. Anaranjado.

Juan: Correct. Perfect!

Chris: Did you dig a ditch?

Juan: Yes. And the crew is tired.

Chris: Let's go eat and drink a lot of water.

Juan: My friends. . . Attention! We're going to eat.
(at two thirty)

Chris: Okay. First, pull the pipe.

Juan: Second, connect the heads?

Chris: That's correct. And install the valves.

Juan: Adjust the valves?

Chris: Yes. And pack the soil.

Juan: Okay. I'm very responsible.

Chris: Yes. You are very hardworking. Thank you.
(at the end of the day)

Chris: Did you connect the pipe?

Juan: Yes.

Chris: Did you install the heads?

Juan: Yes.

Chris: Did you adjust the valves?

Juan: Yes.

Chris: You're nervous, Juan. Are there problems?

Juan: Ah. . . there is. . . there is a leak.

Chris: A leak? Where? Can you work on Sunday?

Chris: Hmmm. . . estudio español. . . *rojo, azul, verde, negro, gris, blanco, café, amarillo, rosado, morado y. . . ana. . . anaran. . .*

Juan: ¡Házlo como yo! A- na -ran- ja- do.

Chris: A-na-ran-ja-do. Anaranjado.

Juan: Correcto. ¡Perfecto!

Chris: ¿Excavaste una zanja?

Juan: Sí. Y la cuadrilla está cansada.

Chris: Vamos a comer y beber mucho agua.

Juan: Amigos. . . ¡Atención ! Vamos a comer.
(a las dos y media)

Chris: Okay. Primero, jala la pipa.

Juan: Segundo, ¿Conecto las cabezas?

Chris: Es correcto. Instala las válvulas.

Juan: ¿Ajusta las válvulas?

Chris: Sí. Y empaca la tierra.

Juan: Está bien. Soy muy responsable.

Chris: Sí. Eres muy trabajador. Gracias.
(al final del día)

Chris: ¿Conectaste la pipa?

Juan: Sí.

Chris: ¿Instalaste las cabezas?

Juan: Sí.

Chris: ¿Ajustaste las válvulas?

Juan: Sí.

Chris: Estás nervioso, Juan. ¿Hay problemas?

Juan: Ah . . . hay . . . hay una fuga.

Chris: ¿Una fuga? ¿Dónde? ¿Puedes trabajar el domingo?

Traduzca al español.

1. How's the family? _____

2. I'm studying Spanish. _____

3. Try it. Keep trying. _____

4. How many pizzas are there? There are four. _____

5. Fantastic! Incredible! Fabulous! _____

6. There are twenty four hours in a day. _____

7. The crew is sensitive. The crew is in a bad mood. _____

8. The woman is the manager. The man is a technician. _____

9. My uncle is responsible. My aunt is hardworking. _____

10. Do you like to play soccer? Where? When? _____

11. My head hurts. Does your ankle hurt? _____

12. Wear your uniform. Wash your uniform. _____

13. Wash and put away the wheelbarrow. _____

14. First, deadhead the white flowers. _____

15. Second, fertilize and water the plants. _____

16. Spread and tamp the soil. Add the mulch. _____

17. Get the red bricks and the gray stones. _____

18. Tag the names. Tag the prices. _____

19. Repot the purple perennials in clay pots. _____

20. Where? Left? Right? Between? Behind? _____

OTROS TERMINOS

pipe sizes	**tamaños de pipa, tubo**	forty-five	**cuarenta y cinco grados**
half inch	**media pulgada**	coupling	**la junta, la conexión**
three quarters	**tres cuartos**	cap	**el casquillo de pipa, tubo**
one inch	**una pulgada**		
one and a quarter	**una y cuarto**	ditch	**la zanja**
one and a half	**una y media**	deep	**profundo, hondo**
two inches	**dos pulgadas**	deeper	**más profundo, más hondo**
three inches	**tres pulgadas**		
pipe fittings	**las conexiones**	shallow	**poco profundo, bajo**
threaded pipe	**la pipa roscada**	wet	**mojado**
nipple	**el niple**	dry	**seco**
elbow	**el codo**	mud	**el lodo**
tee	**la "T"**	above ground	**sobre tierra**
ninety degrees	**el codo de noventa grados**	below ground	**bajo tierra**

LA CULTURA: TRABAJADORES INMIGRANTES

Durante las temporadas de poco desempleo, es difícil conseguir mano de obra. Muchas organizaciones contratan empleados extranjeros. Si un empleador no está seguro acerca de los pasos que debe seguir al contratar a ese tipo de trabajadores, el U.S. Immigration and Naturalization Service (INS) le enviará un manual que explica las normas para esa contratación. Usted puede comunicarse con el INS en la dirección de Internet: *www.usdoj.gov/ins/*.

Las sanciones por contratar "deliberadamente" trabajadores ilegales y ser objeto de una auditoría por parte del INS pueden ser muy severas; por esa razón muchas organizaciones están contratando empleados de México a través del programa H-2B del gobierno de los Estados Unidos. Este programa está dirigido específicamente al empleo temporal y estacional. Conseguir empleados en México es una tarea que consume mucho tiempo y dinero, pero el esfuerzo se justifica a largo plazo.

El proceso tarda aproximadamente 120 días y comprende dos pasos fundamentales: 1) encontrar y reclutar los trabajadores y 2) completar el papeleo para permitirles que vengan a los Estados Unidos y trabajen para su organización.

Una persona puede seguir este proceso sin ayuda, pero se sugiere conseguir la asistencia de profesionales. Hay muchos servicios de empleo según el programa H-2B a la disposición de una organización para reclutar trabajadores latinos y completar el papeleo necesario.

14

El Campo de Golf y La Pesca

PARTE I EL CAMPO DE GOLF

el campo de golf
golf course

las marcas de bola
ball marks

las raspadas
divots

la trampa
bunker

los gansos
geese

la mierda de los gansos
geese poop

las banderas
flags

el hoyo, la copa
hole, cup

el tee de hombres
men's tee

el tee de mujeres
women's tee

los jugadores
players

los miembros
members

el carrito
golf cart

la área de práctica
driving range

la basura
garbage

EJERCICIO DE CORRESPONDENCIA

Escriba la letra de cada dibujo al lado de la palabra inglesa que corresponda abajo.

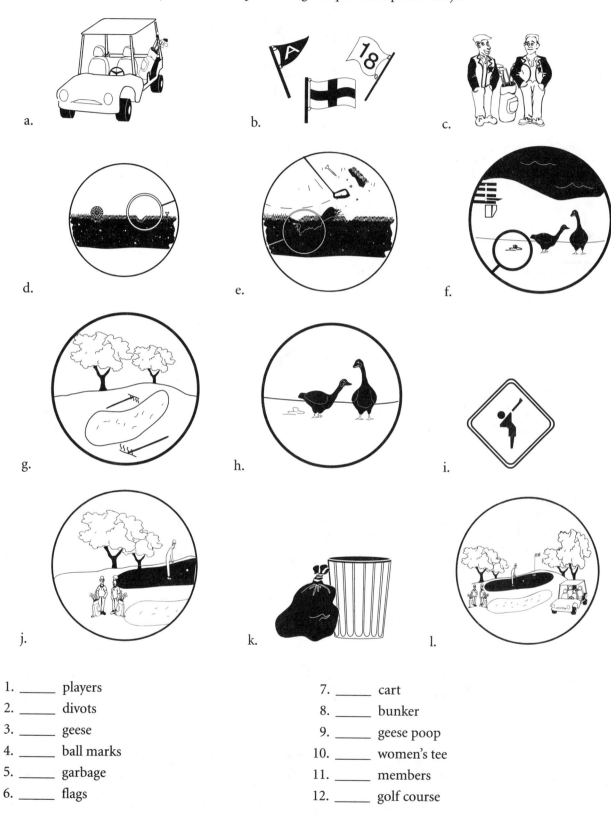

a.

b.

c.

d.

e.

f.

g.

h.

i.

j.

k.

l.

1. _____ players

2. _____ divots

3. _____ geese

4. _____ ball marks

5. _____ garbage

6. _____ flags

7. _____ cart

8. _____ bunker

9. _____ geese poop

10. _____ women's tee

11. _____ members

12. _____ golf course

EJERCICIO DE VOCABULARIO

Escriba la palabra inglesa abajo.

1. _____

2. _____

3. _____

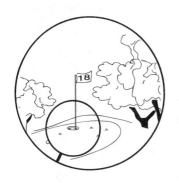

4. _____

5. _____

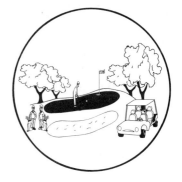

6. _____

7. _____

8. _____

9. _____

10. _____

11. _____

12. _____

EJERCICIO DE CORRESPONDENCIA

Escriba la letra de la palabra en español junto a la palabra inglesa que corresponda a la izquierda.

1. _____ divots
2. _____ bunker
3. _____ men's tee
4. _____ golf course
5. _____ geese
6. _____ ball marks
7. _____ women's tee
8. _____ hole, cup
9. _____ golf cart
10. _____ driving range
11. _____ geese poop
12. _____ players
13. _____ members
14. _____ garbage
15. _____ flags

a. las marcas de bola
b. el carrito
c. la mierda de los gansos
d. las banderas
e. las raspadas
f. el campo de golf
g. los miembros
h. la área de práctica
i. la trampa
j. el hoyo, la copa
k. el tee de hombres
l. la basura
m. el tee de mujeres
n. los gansos
o. los jugadores

CRUCIGRAMAS

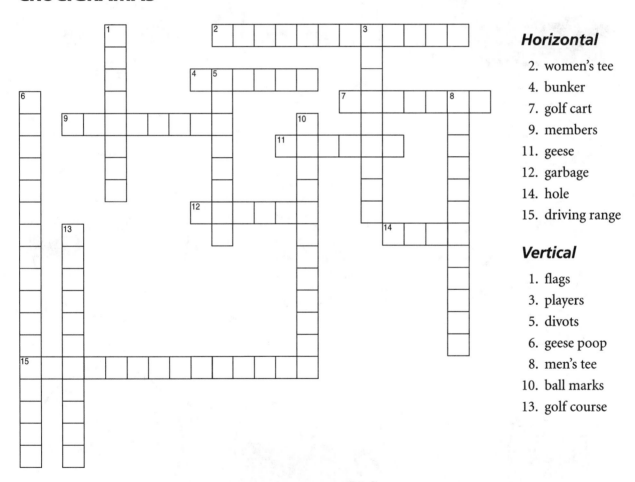

Horizontal

2. women's tee
4. bunker
7. golf cart
9. members
11. geese
12. garbage
14. hole
15. driving range

Vertical

1. flags
3. players
5. divots
6. geese poop
8. men's tee
10. ball marks
13. golf course

Horizontal

4. tee de mujeres
6. jugadores
8. área de practica
10. gansos
11. banderas
12. marcas de bola
13. miembros

Vertical

1. hoyo
2. tee de hombres
3. carrito
5. raspadas
7. basura
9. mierda de los gansos
10. campo de golf
12. trampa

EJERCICIO DE TRADUCCIÓN

Traduzca al inglés.

1. las marcas de bola _____
2. las raspadas _____
3. la trampa _____
4. el tee de hombres _____
5. el campo de golf _____
6. la mierda de los gansos _____
7. los miembros _____
8. el carrito _____
9. el tee de mujeres _____
10. el hoyo, la copa _____
11. los jugadores _____
12. la basura _____
13. los gansos _____
14. la área de práctica _____
15. las banderas _____

Traduzca al español.

1. golf course _____
2. geese poop _____
3. ball marks _____
4. divots _____
5. bunker _____
6. men's tee _____
7. women's tee _____
8. hole, cup _____
9. players _____
10. members _____
11. golf cart _____
12. driving range _____
13. flags _____
14. garbage _____
15. geese _____

OPCIONES MÚLTIPLES

Marque con un círculo la letra de la respuesta correcta.

1. flags
  a. las banderas
  b. los gansos
  c. la basura
  d. las raspadas

2. golf cart
  a. la trampa
  b. la mierda de los gansos
  c. los miembros
  d. el carrito

3. players
  a. los jugadores
  b. los gansos
  c. la basura
  d. las raspadas

4. members
  a. los gansos
  b. los miembros

  c. los jugadores
  d. las raspadas

5. garbage
  a. los jugadores
  b. los gansos
  c. la basura
  d. las raspadas

6. ball marks
  a. las marcas de bola
  b. la trampa
  c. la basura
  d. las raspadas

7. divots
  a. los jugadores
  b. los gansos
  c. la basura
  d. las raspadas

8. bunker
  a. las marcas de bola
  b. las raspadas
  c. la basura
  d. la trampa

9. geese
  a. los jugadores
  b. los gansos
  c. la basura
  d. las raspadas

10. geese poop
  a. la mierda de los gansos
  b. las marcas de bola
  c. los gansos
  d. los miembros

PARTE II   TÉRMINOS DE ACCIÓN

repara	**repair**
recoge	**pick up**
asusta	**scare**
sonríe	**smile**
corta	**cut**
rastrilla	**rake**

EJERCICIO DE CORRESPONDENCIA

Escriba la letra de la palabra en español junto a la palabra inglesa que corresponda a la izquierda.

1. _____ repair   4. _____ smile   a. sonríe   d. asusta

2. _____ pick up   5. _____ cut   b. rastrilla   e. recoge

3. _____ scare   6. _____ rake   c. repara   f. corta

EJERCICIO DE TRADUCCIÓN

Traduzca al inglés.

1. recoge _____

2. corta _____

3. sonríe _____

4. rastrilla _____

5. repara _____

6. asusta _____

Traduzca al español.

1. scare _____

2. smile _____

3. repair _____

4. pick up _____

5. cut _____

6. rake _____

OPCIONES MÚLTIPLES

Marque con un círculo la letra de la respuesta correcta.

1. repair
   a. asusta
   b. recoge
   c. rastrilla
   d. repara

2. pick up
   a. sonríe
   b. recoge
   c. rastrilla
   d. repara

3. scare
   a. asusta
   b. repara
   c. sonríe
   d. recoge

4. cut
   a. repara
   b. recoge
   c. rastrilla
   d. corta

5. smile
   a. repara
   b. asusta
   c. sonríe
   d. recoge

6. rake
   a. corta
   b. recoge
   c. rastrilla
   d. repara

EJERCICIO DE TRADUCCIÓN

Traduzca al inglés.

1. Recoge la basura. _____

2. Corta los hoyos. _____

3. Sonríe a los miembros. _____

4. Rastrilla las trampas. _____

5. Recoge las banderas. _____

6. Repara las raspadas. _____

7. Asusta los gansos. _____

8. Recoge la mierda de los gansos. _____

9. Sonríe a los jugadores. _____

10. Repara las marcas de bola. _____

Traduzca al español.

1. Scare the geese. _____

2. Pick up the geese poop. _____

3. Smile at the members. _____

4. Repair the ball marks. _____

5. Pick up the garbage. _____

6. Cut the holes. _____

7. Rake the bunkers. _____

8. Smile at the players. _____

9. Repair the divots. _____

10. Pick up the flags. _____

EJERCICIO ORAL

¡El Campeonato del Club! ¡Es la semana del torneo y usted quiere que el campo de golf tenga un aspecto fabuloso para los miembros del club y para el comité de golf! Ordene a su empleado que vaya *(Vete a)* a un hoyo en el campo. Entonces su compañero de trabajo le pregunta qué es lo que debe hacer. Sigue el modelo.

STUDENT A:	Go to ten. . .
STUDENT B:	And scare the geese?

1.

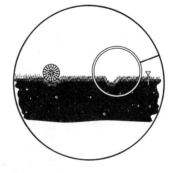

2.

3.

4.

5.

6.

7.

8.

PARTE III   LA PESCA

el barco
boat

el guía
guide

el pez
fish

el pescador
fisherman

la caña
rod

el carrete
reel

el cordel
line

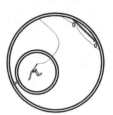

la carnada
bait

el nudo
knot

la red
net

la cámara
camera

el sombrero
hat

las gafas de sol
sunglasses

la mochila
backpack

la toalla
towel

EJERCICIO DE CORRESPONDENCIA

Escriba la letra de cada dibujo al lado de la palabra inglesa que corresponda abajo.

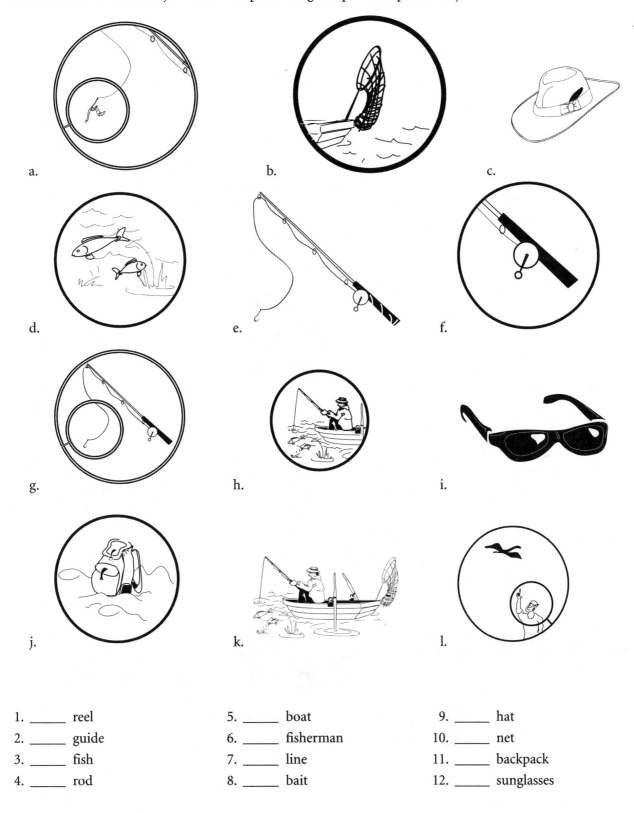

a.

b.

c.

d.

e.

f.

g.

h.

i.

j.

k.

l.

1. _____ reel

2. _____ guide

3. _____ fish

4. _____ rod

5. _____ boat

6. _____ fisherman

7. _____ line

8. _____ bait

9. _____ hat

10. _____ net

11. _____ backpack

12. _____ sunglasses

EJERCICIO DE VOCABULARIO

Escriba la palabra inglesa abajo.

1. _____

2. _____

3. _____

4. _____

5. _____

6. _____

7. _____

8. _____

9. _____

10. _____

11. _____

12. _____

EJERCICIO DE CORRESPONDENCIA

Escriba la letra de la palabra en español junto a la palabra inglesa que corresponda a la izquierda.

1. _____ boat	9. _____ knot	a. la carnada	i. la toalla
2. _____ guide	10. _____ net	b. el cordel	j. el pescador
3. _____ fish	11. _____ camera	c. las gafas de sol	k. el barco
4. _____ fisherman	12. _____ hat	d. la red	l. el pez
5. _____ rod	13. _____ sunglasses	e. la mochila	m. el sombrero
6. _____ reel	14. _____ backpack	f. la caña	n. el carrete
7. _____ line	15. _____ towel	g. el guía	o. la cámara
8. _____ bait		h. el nudo	

CRUCIGRAMAS

Horizontal

3. bait
6. sunglasses
8. camera
11. fisherman
12. boat
13. towel
14. fish

Vertical

1. rod
2. guide
4. knot
5. line
7. hat
9. net
10. reel

Horizontal

2. pez
4. pescador
6. carrete
8. sombrero
9. red
11. mochila
13. cámara
14. toalla

Vertical

1. guía
3. gafas de sol
5. caña
7. cordel
10. barca
11. carnada
12. nudo

EJERCICIO DE TRADUCCIÓN

Traduzca al inglés.

1. el pescador _____
2. la caña _____
3. el cordel _____
4. el barco _____
5. el guía _____
6. el pez _____
7. el sombrero _____
8. la mochila _____
9. las gafas de sol _____
10. la carnada _____
11. el nudo _____
12. la red _____
13. la cámara _____
14. el carrete _____
15. la toalla _____

Traduzca al español.

1. knot _____
2. net _____
3. boat _____
4. guide _____
5. fish _____
6. rod _____
7. reel _____
8. backpack _____
9. towel _____
10. line _____
11. bait _____
12. fisherman _____
13. camera _____
14. hat _____
15. sunglasses _____

OPCIONES MÚLTIPLES

Marque con un círculo la letra de la respuesta correcta.

1. **knot**
   a. la red
   b. la caña
   c. el nudo
   d. la mochila

2. **net**
   a. la caña
   b. el nudo
   c. el barco
   d. la red

3. **boat**
   a. el barco
   b. el cordel
   c. el red
   d. el pez

4. **reel**
   a. la caña
   b. el cordel

   c. la carnada
   d. el carrete

5. **backpack**
   a. la red
   b. la mochila
   c. la carnada
   d. el guía

6. **line**
   a. el cordel
   b. la red
   c. la carnada
   d. la caña

7. **guide**
   a. el pescador
   b. el carrete
   c. el guía
   d. el bote

8. **fish**
   a. la carnada
   b. el pescador
   c. la mochila
   d. el pez

9. **rod**
   a. la caña
   b. la red
   c. el guía
   d. el nudo

10. **bait**
    a. las gafas de sol
    b. la carnada
    c. el carrete
    d. el bote

EJERCICIO ORAL

What do I need? Imagínese que usted está comprando en su tienda favorita, Hayes Bait and Tackle Shop. El vendedor le pregunta qué es lo que usted necesita: *What do you need?* Sigue el modelo.

STUDENT A:	What do you need?
STUDENT B:	I need a reel.

1.

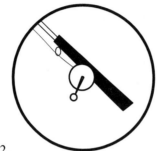

2.

3.

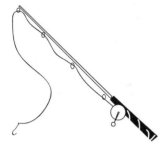

4.

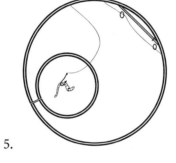

5.

6.

7.

8.

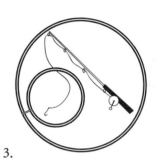

9.

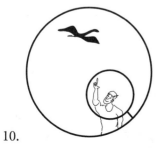

10.

¡Hagamos de todo! ¡Usted y su amigo están planeando su viaje a Cabo San Lucas, en la Baja California! Pregúntele a su compañero cúales actividades le gustaría realizar en las vacaciones. Dígale que usted está de acuerdo. Use: *Yes, let's. . .* (Sí, vamos a. . .). Sigue el modelo.

STUDENT A:	Do you like to play tennis?
STUDENT B:	Yes. Let's play tennis!

1.

2.

3.

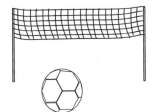

4.

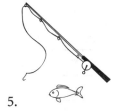

5.

6.

7.

8.

REPASO

Traduzca al inglés.

1. Repara las marcas de bola. _____

2. Vete a la área de practica. _____

3. Asusta los gansos. _____

4. Recoge la basura en el campo de golf. _____

5. Necesito una cámara. ¡Sonríe! _____

6. ¿Qué necesitas? _____

7. Necesito un guía y un bote. _____

8. Repara el carrete. _____

9. Corta el cordel. Corta el nudo. _____

10. ¡La red! ¡La red! ¡La cámara! _____

Traduzca al español.

1. Repair the ball marks and the divots. _____

2. Smile at the members and players. _____

3. Scare the geese. _____

4. Pick up the garbage and the goose poop. _____

5. Go to the women's tee. _____

6. Cut the holes. Rake the bunkers. _____

7. What do you need? _____

8. I need a hat and sunglasses. _____

9. I need a rod, reel, line, and bait. _____

10. I need the net and the camera! _____

*Lea el diálogo en voz alta en inglés.
Seguidamente tradúzcalo al español.*

(in the store, Live Bait)

Peter: Welcome, Walt! How's it going?

Walt: Exceptional! We're going to Mexico on
February seventeenth.

Danny: Yes… we're going fishing. Are there many
fish in Cabo San Lucas?

Peter: Yes. And in February and March there are
marlin and tuna. What do you need?

Walt: I need a rod and reel.

Peter: Come with me, Walt.

Walt: And line… my line is in knots.

Peter: (shows the correct way) Watch me. Do it
like me.

Walt: Okay… okay. Thanks, Pete.

Peter: See you later.

(on the streets of Cabo San Lucas)

Danny: First, to the hotel.

Walt: No… no. First to the golf course!

Danny: No. First to the bank.

Walt: Good idea. You're very responsible, Dan.

Danny: And I study Spanish! Watch me… excuse
me, ma'am…

(Danny is speaking Spanish with the woman.)

Woman: Yes? What do you need?

Danny: Help me, please…Where is the
bank?

Woman: Do you need a taxi or a guide?

Danny: No, thank you.

Woman: It's around here… it's near…

Danny: Is it behind the church?

Woman: Yes, it's between Benito Juarez Street and
Fox Avenue.

Danny: Thank you.

(el Dorado Golf Course)

Walt: A reservation for two players, please.

*Lea el diálogo en voz alta en español.
Seguidamente tradúzcalo al inglés.*

(en la tienda, Live Bait)

Peter: Bienvenidos, Walt! ¿Qué tal?

Walt: ¡Excepcional! Vamos a Méjico el diez y siete
de febrero.

Danny: Sí… vamos a pescar. ¿Hay muchos peces
en Cabo San Lucas?

Peter: Sí. Y en febrero y marzo hay marlin y atún.
¿Qué necesitas?

Walt: Necesito una caña y un carrete.

Peter: Ven conmigo, Walt.

Walt: Y cordel… mi cordel está en nudos.

Peter: (le muestra la manera correcta) Mírame.
Házlo como yo.

Walt: Okay… okay. Gracias, Pete.

Peter: Hasta luego.

(en las calles de Cabo San Lucas)

Danny: Primero… al hotel.

Walt: No… no. ¡Primero al campo de golf!

Danny: No. Primero al banco.

Walt: Buena idea. Eres muy responsable, Dan.

Danny: ¡Y estudio español! Mírame… perdón,
señora…

(Danny habla español con la mujer.)

Woman: ¿Sí? ¿Qué necesitas?

Danny: Ayúdame, por favor… ¿Dónde está el
banco?

Woman: ¿Necesitas un taxi o un guía?

Danny: No, gracias.

Woman : Está por aquí… está cerca…

Danny: ¿Está detrás de la iglesia?

Woman : Sí, está entre las calles Benito Juarez y la
Avenida Fox.

Danny: Gracias.

(el Campo de Golf el Dorado)

Walt: Una reservación para dos jugadores, por favor.

Ignacio: What day, sir?

Walt: On Thursday, Friday, and Saturday.

Danny: On Saturday, no, Walt. We're going fishing on Saturday.

Walt: Oh, yes…you are very organized, Dan.

Ignacio: At what time do you want to play on Thursday and on Friday?

Walt: At ten o'clock, please.

(on Thursday, 8:30 A.M.)

Danny: Good morning, Walt.

Walt: Aaahhh…

Danny: How are you? You're not well?

Walt: I'm sick…

Danny: What hurts?

Walt: My stomach and my head hurt.

Danny: Many margaritas, music, and women?

Walt: I'm tired…

Danny: Let's go! Let's go eat, Walt.

Ignacio: ¿Qué días, señor?

Walt: El jueves, viernes, y sábado.

Danny: El sábado, no, Walt. Vamos a pescar el sábado.

Walt: Ah, sí . . . eres muy organizado, Dan.

Ignacio: ¿A qué hora te gusta jugar el jueves y el viernes?

Walt: A las diez, por favor.

(el jueves a las ocho y media)

Danny: Buenos días, Walt.

Walt: Aaahhh. . .

Danny: ¿Cómo estás? ¿No estás bien?

Walt: Estoy enfermo. . .

Danny: ¿Qué te duele?

Walt: Me duele el estómago y la cabeza.

Danny: ¿Muchas margaritas, música, y mujeres?

Walt: Estoy cansado. . .

Danny: ¡Vamos! Vamos a comer, Walt.

Traduzca al español.

1. I'm nervous. I'm busy. I'm in a good mood. _____

2. Are you sick or tired? _____

3. The party is Tuesday, October 7. There is pizza and beer. _____

4. What do you like to do? Bowl or play billiards? _____

5. It's bad. Get the first aid kit. _____

6. What hurts? Your eye? Your ear? _____

7. Give me the lawnmower. Mix the oil and gas. _____

8. Where is the gas chainsaw? _____

9. Prune the trees and the shrubs. _____

10. Blow and rake the leaves. _____

11. Load the soil and pine straw. _____

12. Deadhead and fertilize the red annuals. _____

13. Weed the hanging baskets. _____

14. Put the trees in the back yard near the pond. _____

15. Dig a ditch and install the pipe. _____

LA CULTURA: CONSEJOS PARA LOS VIAJES

Dos personas han decidido trabajar en los Estados Unidos. Una de ellas se deprime y la otra tiene una experiencia muy interesante y agradable. ¿Cómo se explica esta diferencia en sus respectivas experiencias?

Está claro que las ideas, actitudes y expectativas que la gente procedente de otros países trae consigo a los Estados Unidos, así como su conocimiento de la sociedad y la cultura estadounidenses, tienen una gran influencia sobre la naturaleza de la experiencia que viven en este país. Esperamos que las secciones culturales de los capítulos anteriores le hayan ayudado a comprender aspectos de la cultura de los Estados Unidos en relación con su propia cultura. Sin embargo, es posible que usted sienta de todos modos un choque cultural, pero ya lo superará. Le deseamos lo mejor a usted y a su familia así como a todos nuestros grandes países.

A continuación le presentamos algunos otros aspectos que hay que tener en cuenta al comenzar a viajar por los Estados Unidos.

Clima

En general, el clima de los Estados Unidos es templado, con cuatro estaciones bien diferenciadas. La mitad norte del país tiene típicamente nieve en el invierno. Los meses más fríos son diciembre, enero y febrero; siendo los meses más cálidos los de junio, julio y agosto.

Dinero

Como usted sabe, la moneda de los Estados Unidos es el dólar. Viene en billetes con denominaciones de 1, 2 (no es común), 5, 10, 20, 50 y 100. Ten cuidado con los billetes. Tienen todos el mismo tamaño y color. Las monedas tienen nombres especiales. Esos nombres son:

1 centavo	**penny**
5 centavos	**nickel**
10 centavos	**dime**
25 centavos	**quarter**
50 centavos	**medio dólar (half-dollar)**

Usted no debe llevar consigo gran cantidad de dinero en efectivo. Compre cheques de viajero en dólares antes de salir de su país. Estos cheques de viajero son aceptados en casi todas las partes.

La gente en los Estados Unidos no guarda mucho dinero en sus carteras o en sus casas. Su dinero está mucho más seguro en un banco. Confíe en que su empleador o patrón quiere ayudarle en este asunto. Pídale que abra una cuenta para usted con el banco de la compañía y pregúntele cómo usar correctamente una tarjeta de crédito. Es bueno tener una tarjeta de crédito, pero nunca abuse de ella, puesto que puede caer en terribles deudas.

Si usted desea enviar dinero a su casa por correo, puede usar el Servicio Postal de los Estados Unidos. Pregunte cómo enviar un giro postal internacional. Usted también puede transferir dinero a un banco en su país. O usar los servicios de una casa de cambio de moneda en su nueva ciudad.

Leyes Sobre Bebidas Alcohólicas

En los Estados Unidos hay una ley que prohibe que personas menores de 21 años beban o compren bebidas alcohólicas; por esa razón a usted le pueden pedir que demuestre su edad con algún documento. Usted debe tener 21 o más años de edad.

Usted debe tener en cuenta que hay leyes extremadamente rigurosas contra el consumo de bebidas alcohólicas antes o durante la conducción de un automóvil. Es ilegal tener una botella o lata abierta de alcohol en un vehículo. Usted perderá su permiso de conducir. En algunos lugares públicos como, por ejemplo, playas y parques, usted no puede beber alcohol. Para prevenir que la gente muera en accidentes automovilísticos, se han acuñado algunas nuevas frases comunes. "Los amigos no dejan que los amigos conduzcan borrachos" y "Si usted bebe, ¡no conduzca!" Es muy común tener un "conductor designado" para la velada. Esta persona no beberá alcohol y llevará a sus amigos a sus respectivas casas con seguridad. También, hay una ley que dice que es ilegal llevar consigo cuchillos y pistolas en los Estados Unidos.

abajo	**down, below**	amarillo	**yellow**
el abono	**compost**	aquí	**here**
abre	**open**	los árboles	**trees**
abril	**April**	los arbustos	**shrubs**
los abuelos	**grandparents**	la área de práctica	**driving range**
el aceite	**oil**	la arena	**sand**
adiós	**goodbye**	argentino (a)	**Argentine**
agarra	**hold**	arriba	**up, above**
agosto	**August**	asusta	**scare**
agresivo, a	**aggressive**	¡Atención!	**Attention!**
el agua	**water**	¡Aviso!	**Warning!**
ajusta	**adjust**	ayer	**yesterday**
el alambre	**wire**	azul	**blue**
la alberca	**pool**	el banco	**bank**
allá	**over there**	las banderas	**flags**
allí	**there**	la banqueta	**sidewalk**
alrededor	**around**	el barco	**boat**
ambicioso, a	**ambitious**	barre	**sweep**
los amigos	**friends**	el barro	**clay**
añade	**add**	la basura	**garbage**
anaranjado	**orange**	la biblioteca	**library**
el año	**year**	bienvenidos	**welcome**
las anuales	**annuals**	blanco	**white**
el aparcamiento	**parking lot**	boliviano (a)	**Bolivian**
los apartamentos	**apartments**	la boquilla	**nozzle**
aplica	**apply**	las botas	**boots**

el botiquín	**first aid kit**	conecta	**connect**
el brazo	**arm**	confundido, a	**confused**
la cabeza	**head**	consigue	**get**
las cabezas	**sprinkler heads**	cooperativo, a	**cooperative**
café	**brown**	contento, a	**content**
la caja	**box**	el cordel	**line**
¡Caliente!	**Hot!**	corta	**cut**
la calle	**street**	corta la mala	**deadhead**
la calzada	**driveway**	el cortado	**clippings**
la cámara	**camera**	la corteza	**bark**
el campo de golf	**golf course**	pon en costal	**burlap**
la caña	**rod**	cruel	**cruel**
cansado, a	**tired**	la cuadrilla	**crew**
las canastas colgadas	**hanging baskets**	cuándo	**when**
carga	**load**	cubano (a)	**Cuban**
la carnada	**bait**	el cuello	**neck**
la carretilla	**wheelbarrow**	dentro	**inside**
el carrete	**reel**	derecha	**right**
el carrito	**cart**	detrás	**behind**
la casa	**house**	descarga	**unload**
el casco de seguridad	**safety helmet**	deshierba	**weed**
el cemento	**cement**	el día	**day**
el cementerio	**cemetery**	diciembre	**December**
cepilla	**brush**	domingo	**Sunday**
el cepillo	**push broom**	dominicano (a)	**Dominican**
cerca	**near**	dónde	**where**
la cerca	**fence**	los dedos	**fingers**
checa	**check**	ecuatoriano (a)	**Ecuadorian**
chileno (a)	**Chilean**	el edificio	**building**
cierra	**close**	empaca	**pack**
el cliente	**customer**	empuja	**push**
el codo	**elbow**	en	**in, on**
cómico, a	**comical**	encima	**on top**
cómo	**how**	enero	**January**

enfermo, a	**sick**	furioso, a	**furious**
en punto	**exactly, sharp**	las gafas de sol	**sunglasses**
enojado, a	**angry**	los galones	**gallons**
entre	**between**	los gansos	**geese**
envuelve	**wrap**	el garaje	**garage**
empareja	**spread**	la gasolina	**gas**
la escoba	**broom**	generoso, a	**generous**
la escuela	**school**	el (la) gerente	**manager**
la espalda	**back**	gracias	**thank you**
la esposa	**wife**	gris	**grey**
el esposo	**husband**	los guantes	**gloves**
estadounidense	**United States citizen**	guarda	**put away**
el estanque	**pond**	guatemalteco (a)	**Guatemalan**
este	**east**	el guía	**guide**
el estómago	**stomach**	haz bola	**ball**
las etiquetas	**tags, labels**	las hierbas	**weeds**
excava	**dig**	la hija	**daughter**
¡Excelente!	**Excellent!**	el hijo	**son**
¡Excepcional!	**Exceptional!**	los hijos	**children**
el extinguidor	**fire extinguisher**	la hermana	**sister**
extrovertido, a	**extroverted**	el hermano	**brother**
¡Fabuloso!	**Fabulous!**	las hojas	**leaves**
la familia	**family**	hola	**hi/hello**
¡Fantástico!	**Fantastic!**	hondureño (a)	**Honduran**
por favor	**please**	honesto, a	**honest**
el fertilizante	**fertilizer**	el hombre	**man**
febrero	**February**	el hombro	**shoulder**
feliz	**happy**	la horca	**pitchfork**
el fin de semana	**weekend**	el hospital	**hospital**
el flat	**flat**	el hotel	**hotel**
las flores	**flowers**	hoy	**today**
la fuente	**fountain**	el hoyo	**hole**
fuera	**outside**	el hoyo, la copa	**hole, cup**
la fuga	**leak**	la iglesia	**church**

impaciente	**impatient**	mañana por la noche	**tomorrow night**
impulsivo, a	**impulsive**	la manguera	**hose**
independiente	**independent**	la mano	**hand**
instala	**install**	la máquina	**lawnmower**
intelectual	**intellectual**	¡Maravilloso!	**Marvelous!**
inteligente	**intelligent**	el marro, el mazo	**sledge hammer**
introvertido, a	**introverted**	martes	**Tuesday**
el invierno	**winter**	marzo	**March**
izquierda	**left**	materialisto, a	**materialistic**
jala	**pull**	mayo	**May**
el jardín de atrás	**back yard**	el mayordomo	**foreman, crew leader**
el jardín de enfrente	**front yard**	el mecánico	**technician**
el jefe	**boss**	mexicano (a)	**Mexican**
jueves	**Thursday**	el mes	**month**
los jugadores	**players**	la mesa de plantar	**potting bench**
julio	**July**	mezcla	**mix**
junio	**June**	la mezcla	**mulch (mixture)**
justo, a	**fair**	miércoles	**Wednesday**
lava	**wash**	los miembros	**members**
lejos	**far**	la mierda de los gansos	**geese poop**
los ladrillos	**bricks**	la mochila	**backpack**
la lata	**can**	el montón	**pile**
las llantas	**tires**	morado	**purple**
los lentes de seguridad	**safety glasses**	mueve	**move**
limpia	**clean**	muele	**mulch**
lunes	**Monday**	la mujer	**woman**
el mall	**shopping mall**	negro	**black**
la maceta	**pot**	nervioso, a	**nervous**
la madre	**mother**	nicaragüense	**Nicaraguan**
¡Magnífico!	**Magnificent!**	noche	**night**
mañana	**tomorrow**	los nombres	**names**
mañana	**morning**	norte	**north**
mañana por la tarde	**tomorrow afternoon**	noviembre	**November**
mañana por la mañana	**tomorrow morning**	el nudo	**knot**

ocupado, a	**busy**	poda	**prune**
octubre	**October**	la podadera	**pruner**
oeste	**west**	pon	**put, tag**
el oído	**ear**	pon en costal	**burlap**
el ojo	**eye**	por qué	**why**
organizado, a	**organized**	preocupado, a	**worried**
el otoño	**fall**	los precios	**prices**
paciente	**patient**	prepara	**prepare**
el padre	**father**	la primavera	**spring**
los padres	**parents**	primero	**first**
la paleta	**pallet**	el (la) primo(a)	**cousin**
panameño (a)	**Panamanian**	la puerta	**gate**
la paja	**pine straw**	puertorriqueño (a)	**Puerto Rican**
la pala	**shovel**	las pulgadas	**inches**
paraguayo (a)	**Paraguayan**	qué	**what**
el parque	**park**	¡Quema!	**Burns!**
el patio	**patio**	quién	**who**
el pecho	**chest**	las raíces	**roots**
¡Peligro!	**Danger!**	las ramas	**branches**
¡Perfecto!	**Perfect!**	las raspadas	**divots**
las perennes	**perennials**	la rastrilla	**rake**
el perro	**dog**	el rastrillo de tierra	**soil rake**
peruano (a)	**Peruvian**	el rastrillo de hojas	**leaf rake**
el pescador	**fisherman**	el recipiente	**container**
el pez	**fish**	riega	**water**
el pico	**pick**	recoge	**pick up**
las piedras	**stones**	la red	**net**
la pierna	**leg**	reemplaza	**replace**
los pies	**feet**	regresa	**return**
la pipa	**pipe**	repara	**repair**
planta	**plant**	replanta	**repot**
planta	**pot, to**	responsable	**responsible**
las plantas	**plants**	el restaurante	**restaurant**
la plastalina	**clay**	la roca	**rock**

rocía	**spray**	los tapones para los oídos	**earplugs**
el rociador	**sprinkler**	tarde	**afternoon**
la rodilla	**knee**	tarde	**late**
rojo	**red**	temprano	**early**
romántico, a	**romantic**	el tee de hombres	**men's tee**
rosado	**pink**	el tee de mujeres	**women's tee**
el rototiller	**rototiller**	tercero	**third**
sábado	**Saturday**	la tía	**aunt**
saca	**take out**	a tiempo	**on time**
saca el agua	**flush**	la tienda	**store**
el saco	**bag**	la tierra	**soil**
la sangre	**blood**	tímido, a	**timid**
salvadoreño (a)	**Salvadorian**	el tío	**uncle**
segundo	**second**	la toalla	**towel**
la secretaria	**secretary**	el tobillo	**ankle**
la semana	**week**	trabajador / trabajadora	**hardworking**
las semillas	**seeds**	trae	**bring**
sensible	**sensitive**	la trampa	**bunker**
el sendero	**path**	triste	**sad**
septiembre	**September**	la turba	**peat moss**
el serrucho de gas	**gas chainsaw**	el uniforme	**uniform**
sincero, a	**sincere**	la universidad	**university**
sobre	**over**	uruguayo (a)	**Uruguayan**
sociable	**sociable**	usa	**use**
el sol	**sun**	la válvula	**valve**
solamente	**only**	el vecino	**neighbor**
sonríe	**smile**	viernes	**Friday**
la sombra	**shade**	venezolano (a)	**Venezuelan**
el sombrero	**hat**	el verano	**summer**
sopla	**blow**	verde	**green**
la sopladora	**blower**	las yardas	**yards**
Soy . . .	**I'm . . .**	el zacate, el pasto	**grass**
supersticioso, a	**superstitious**	el zacate	**sod**
sur	**south**	la zanja	**trench**

add	**añade**	ball	**haz bola**
adjust	**ajusta**	ball marks	**las marcas de bola**
afternoon	**tarde**	bank	**el banco**
aggressive	**agresivo, a**	bark	**la corteza**
ambitious	**ambicioso, a**	baseball cap	**la gorra**
angry	**enojado, a**	behind	**detrás**
ankle	**el tobillo**	between	**entre**
annuals	**las anuales**	black	**negro**
apartments	**los apartamentos**	blood	**la sangre**
April	**abril**	blow	**sopla**
apply	**aplica**	blower	**la sopladora**
Argentine	**argentino (a)**	blue	**azul**
arm	**el brazo**	boat	**el barco**
around	**alrededor**	Bolivian	**boliviano (a)**
around here	**por aquí**	boots	**las botas**
at night	**por la noche**	boss	**el jefe**
Attention!	**¡Atención!**	box	**la caja**
August	**agosto**	branches	**las ramas**
aunt	**la tía**	bricks	**los ladrillos**
bad mood	**de mal humor**	bring	**trae**
back	**la espalda**	broom	**la escoba**
backpack	**la mochila**	brother	**el hermano**
back yard	**el jardín de atrás**	brown	**café**
bait	**la carnada**	brush	**cepilla**
bag	**el saco**	brush	**el cepillo**

bunker	**la trampa**	Danger!	**¡Peligro!**
building	**el edificio**	day	**el día**
Burns!	**¡Quema!**	daughter	**la hija**
burlap	**pon en costal**	deadhead	**corta la mala**
busy	**ocupado, a**	December	**diciembre**
camera	**la cámara**	dig	**excava**
can	**la lata**	dig up	**saca**
car trunk	**el baúl**	divots	**las raspadas**
cart	**el carrito**	dog	**el perro**
cement	**el cemento**	Dominican	**dominicano (a)**
cemetery	**el cementerio**	down, below	**abajo**
check	**checa**	driveway	**la calzada**
chest	**el pecho**	driving range	**la área de práctica**
children	**los hijos**	ear	**el oído**
Chilean	**chileno (a)**	earplugs	**los tapones para los oídos**
church	**la iglesia**		
clay	**el barro**	early	**temprano**
clean	**limpia**	east	**este**
clippings	**el cortado**	Ecuadorian	**ecuatoriano (a)**
close	**cerca**	elbow	**el codo**
comical	**cómico, a**	exactly, sharp	**en punto**
compost	**el abono**	Excellent!	**¡Excelente!**
confused	**confundido, a**	Exceptional!	**¡Excepcional!**
connect	**conecta**	extroverted	**extrovertido, a**
container	**el recipiente**	eye	**el ojo**
content	**contento, a**	Fabulous!	**¡Fabuloso!**
cooperative	**cooperativo, a**	fair	**justo, a**
Costa Rican	**costarricense**	fall	**el otoño**
cousin	**el (la) primo(a)**	family	**la familia**
crew	**la cuadrilla**	Fantastic!	**¡Fantástico!**
cruel	**cruel**	far	**lejos**
Cuban	**cubano (a)**	father	**el padre**
customer	**el (la) cliente**	February	**febrero**
cut	**corta**	feet	**los pies**

fence	**la cerca**	grass	**el zacate, el pasto**
fertilizer	**el fertilizante**	green	**verde**
fingers	**los dedos**	grey	**gris**
fire extinguisher	**el extinguidor**	Guatemalan	**guatemalteco (a)**
first	**primero**	guide	**el guía**
first aid kit	**el botiquín**	happy	**feliz**
fish	**el pez**	hardworking	**trabajador / trabajadora**
fisherman	**el pescador**		
flags	**las banderas**	hand	**la mano**
flat	**el flat**	hanging baskets	**las canastas colgadas**
flowers	**las flores**	hat	**el sombrero**
flush	**saca el agua**	head	**la cabeza**
foreman, crew leader	**el mayordomo**	here	**aquí**
fountain	**la fuente**	hi/hello	**hola**
Friday	**viernes**	hold	**agarra**
friends	**los amigos**	hole, cup	**el hoyo, la copa**
front yard	**el jardín de enfrente**	Honduran	**hondureño (a)**
furious	**furioso, a**	honest	**honesto, a**
gallons	**los galones**	hose	**la manguera**
garage	**el garaje**	hospital	**el hospital**
garbage	**la basura**	Hot!	**¡Caliente!**
gas	**la gasolina**	hotel	**el hotel**
gas chainsaw	**el serrucho de gas**	house	**la casa**
gate	**la puerta**	how	**cómo**
geese	**los gansos**	husband	**el esposo**
geese poop	**la mierda de los gansos**	I am. . .	**Estoy. . .**
		I'm . . .	**Soy . . .**
generous	**generoso, a**	impatient	**impaciente**
get	**consigue**	impulsive	**impulsivo, a**
gloves	**los guantes**	inches	**las pulgadas**
golf cart	**el carrito**	in the afternoon	**por la tarde**
golf course	**el campo de golf**	in the morning	**por la mañana**
goodbye	**adiós**	independent	**independiente**
grandparents	**los abuelos**	in front	**delante**

in, on	**en**	morning	**mañana**
inside	**dentro**	mother	**la madre**
install	**instala**	move	**mueve**
intellectual	**intelectual**	mulch	**muele**
intelligent	**inteligente**	mulch (mixture)	**la mezcla**
introverted	**introvertido, a**	names	**los nombres**
January	**enero**	near	**cerca**
June	**junio**	neck	**el cuello**
July	**julio**	neighbor	**el vecino**
knee	**la rodilla**	net	**la red**
knot	**el nudo**	nervous	**nervioso, a**
late	**tarde**	Nicaraguan	**nicaragüense**
lawnmower	**la máquina**	night	**noche**
leaf rake	**el rastrillo de hojas**	north	**norte**
leak	**la fuga**	November	**noviembre**
leaves	**las hojas**	nozzle	**la boquilla**
left	**izquierda**	October	**octubre**
leg	**la pierna**	oil	**el aceite**
library	**la biblioteca**	on time	**a tiempo**
line	**el cordel**	on top	**encima**
load	**carga**	only	**solamente**
Magnificent!	**¡Magnífico!**	open	**abre**
man	**el hombre**	over	**sobre**
manager	**el (la) gerente**	over there	**allá**
March	**marzo**	orange	**anaranjado**
Marvelous!	**¡Maravilloso!**	organized	**organizado, a**
materialistic	**materialisto, a**	outside	**fuera**
May	**mayo**	pack	**empaca**
members	**los miembros**	pallet	**la paleta**
men's tee	**el tee de hombres**	Panamanian	**panameño (a)**
Mexican	**mexicano (a)**	Paraguayan	**paraguayo (a)**
mix	**mezcla**	parents	**los padres**
Monday	**lunes**	park	**el parque**
month	**el mes**	parking lot	**el aparcamiento**

path	el sendero	push broom	el cepillo
patient	paciente	put away	guarda
patio	el patio	put, tag	pon
peat moss	la turba	rake	la rastrilla
perennials	las perennes	red	rojo
Perfect!	¡Perfecto!	reel	el carrete
Peruvian	peruano (a)	repair	repara
pick	el pico	replace	reemplaza
pick up	recoge	repot	replanta
pile	el montón	responsible	responsable
pine straw	la paja	restaurant	el restaurante
pink	rosado	return	regresa
pipe	la pipa	right	derecha
pitchfork	la horca	rock	la roca
play, to	jugar	rod	la caña
players	los jugadores	romantic	romántico, a
plant	planta	roots	las raíces
plants	las plantas	rototiller	el rototiller
please	por favor	sad	triste
pond	el estanque	safety helmet	el casco de seguridad
pool	la alberca	safety glasses	los lentes de seguridad
pot (plastic, clay)	la maceta (de plástico, de barro)	Salvadorian	salvadoreño (a)
pot	la maceta	sand	la arena
pot, to	planta	Saturday	sábado
potting bench	la mesa de plantar	scare	asusta
prepare	prepara	school	la escuela
prices	los precios	second	segundo
prune	poda	secretary	la secretaria
pruner	la podadera	seeds	las semillas
Puerto Rican	puertorriqueño (a)	sensitive	sensible
pull	jala	September	septiembre
purple	morado	shade	la sombra
push	empuja	shopping mall	el mall

shoulder	**el hombro**	there	**allí**
shovel	**la pala**	third	**tercero**
shrubs	**los arbustos**	Thursday	**jueves**
sick	**enfermo, a**	timid	**tímido, a**
sidewalk	**la banqueta**	tired	**cansado, a**
sincere	**sincero, a**	tires	**las llantas**
sister	**la hermana**	today	**hoy**
sledge hammer	**el marro, el mazo**	tomorrow	**mañana**
smile	**sonríe**	tomorrow afternoon	**mañana por la tarde**
sociable	**sociable**	tomorrow morning	**mañana por la mañana**
sod	**el zacate**		
soil	**la tierra**	tomorrow night	**mañana por la noche**
soil rake	**el rastrillo de tierra**	towel	**la toalla**
son	**el hijo**	trees	**los árboles**
south	**sur**	trench	**la zanja**
spray	**rocía**	Tuesday	**martes**
spread	**empareja**	uncle	**el tío**
spring	**la primavera**	uniform	**el uniforme**
sprinkler	**el rocíador**	United States citizen	**estadounidense**
sprinkler heads	**las cabezas**	unload	**descarga**
stomach	**el estómago**	university	**la universidad**
stones	**las piedras**	up, above	**arriba**
store	**la tienda**	Uruguayan	**uruguayo (a)**
street	**la calle**	use	**usa**
summer	**el verano**	valve	**la válvula**
sun	**el sol**	Venezuelan	**venezolano (a)**
sunglasses	**las gafas de sol**	Warning!	**¡Aviso!**
Sunday	**domingo**	wash	**lava**
superstitious	**supersticioso, a**	water	**el agua**
sweep	**barre**	watering	**riega**
tags, labels	**las etiquetas**	Wednesday	**miércoles**
take out	**saca**	weed	**deshierba**
technician	**el mecánico**	weeds	**las hierbas**
thank you	**gracias**	week	**la semana**

weekend	**el fin de semana**	wife	**la esposa**
welcome	**bienvenidos**	winter	**el invierno**
west	**oeste**	wire	**el alambre**
what	**qué**	woman	**la mujer**
wheelbarrow	**la carretilla**	women's tee	**el tee de mujeres**
where	**dónde**	worried	**preocupado, a**
where is	**dónde está**	wrap	**envuelve**
when	**cuándo**	yards	**las yardas**
white	**blanco**	year	**el año**
who	**quién**	yellow	**amarillo**
who, what, where	**quién, qué, dónde**	yesterday	**ayer**
why	**por qué**		